Do you . . .

. . . pray your baby will sleep through the night?

. . . wish she'd stay this age forever?

. . . ever think, *Why are there three of us in bed?*

. . . chuckle at the thought that your four-year-old would make a good courtroom attorney someday?

. . . wonder why "she looked at me" is a criminal offense?

. . . find yourself muttering, "Nine-year-olds don't need cell phones"?

. . . wish you could understand that unfathomable feminine mind better?

. . . wonder what "I'll be ready in a minute" really means?

. . . struggle with the concept that her hair is close to sacred?

. . . feel like Judge Judy or Dr. Phil should be on retainer?

. . . wonder why it's so important that a shirt matches the rest of an outfit, and why she needs twenty-two pairs of shoes when you only have three?

. . . have to extract your toothbrush from the tangle of curling irons, hair flatteners, extensions, scrunchies, and other do-jobbies in the bathroom?

. . . wish you had a definition for the word *whatever*?

. . . hope you discover gold in your backyard so you can pay for her upcoming college education?

. . . want to put in for a job that requires lots of travel to avoid her dizzying mood swings?

. . . ever wonder why her "coffee" costs $3.60 a cup?

. . . lie awake at night fearing your daughter will bring home a Loser, with a capital *L*?

. . . question what makes a $400 dress better than a $40 one? (After all, they use about the same amount of material.)

. . . believe your daughter could win Olympic gold in eye-rolling?

. . . dream up a new design every week for a man cave in the garage?

. . . feel like General Custer some Friday nights—making your "Last Stand"?

Dad, with just a little effort on your part, you can gain the kind of relationship you dream of with your daughter—one based on mutual love and respect. Your daughter needs you to help her forge a successful path in life. Her self-esteem, choices, behavior, character, and even her ideas about a marriage partner are all directly tied to you. If you follow the simple suggestions in *Be the Dad She Needs You to Be*, you will be transformed into the kind of man your daughter needs you to be . . . for a lifetime.

BE THE DAD
She Needs You to Be

BE THE DAD
She Needs
You to Be

The Indelible Imprint
a Father Leaves on His Daughter's Life

DR. KEVIN LEMAN

W PUBLISHING GROUP

AN IMPRINT OF THOMAS NELSON

Published in Nashville, Tennessee, by W Publishing Group. W Publishing is a
registered trademark of Thomas Nelson, Inc.

Thomas Nelson titles may be purchased in bulk for educational, business,
fund-raising, or sales promotional use. For information, please e-mail
SpecialMarkets@ThomasNelson.com.

To protect the privacy of those who have shared their stories with the author,
some details and names have been changed.

Any Internet addresses, phone numbers, or company or product information
printed in this book are offered as a resource and are not intended in any
way to be or to imply an endorsement by Thomas Nelson, nor does Thomas
Nelson vouch for the existence, content, or services of these sites, phone
numbers, companies, or products beyond the life of this book.

ISBN: 978-0-529-12332-9 (HC)
ISBN: 978-0-7180-9702-8 (TP)
ISBN: 978-0-7180-1150-5 (ITPE)
ISBN: 978-0-7180-4241-7 (custom)

Library of Congress Control Number: 2013922628

Printed in the United States of America

17 18 19 20 21 LSC 6 5 4 3 2 1

To my four daughters—
Holly, Krissy, Hannah, Lauren—
I love you.
Being a dad is the best gig I ever got.
You've each given me great joy in your own unique way.
May the good Lord bless and keep you.
I know we'll live in each other's hearts forever.

Contents

Acknowledgments

Thanks to . . .

My beloved wife, Sande, whose wisdom about rearing daughters has rubbed off on me.

All those whose questions about dads and daughters sparked the inspiration for *Be the Dad She Needs You to Be*—my book readers, Facebook fans, seminar participants, television watchers, and radio listeners across North America and beyond. Nothing gives me more joy than serving you by providing simple, practical solutions to fine-tune your family relationships.

Debbie Wickwire, senior acquisitions editor at Thomas Nelson, for her passion and enthusiasm for the subject.

My editor, Ramona Cramer Tucker, for her well-honed publishing talents as well as the joy of watching her husband, Jeff, be a great daddy to their daughter, Kayla.

Introduction

Daughters Are a Little Weird (And Even When They're Not Weird, They're a Little Strange)

The quote "Men are from Mars, and women are from Venus" is right on the mark, but that doesn't mean you can't find common ground as dad and daughter.

I hate to admit this in public, because it's a little embarrassing to a manly man, but I can think like a woman. I can get behind a woman's eyes and feel her emotions. It's probably because I've been surrounded by seven women the majority of my life—my mother, my sister, my wife, and my four daughters—and how they think and feel has rubbed off on me. Dad, trust me on this: your daughter sees life completely different than you do. That's why you need to read this book, so you can enter your daughter's world in an informed way and make the kind of imprint only you can make on her life. There are certain things that are very different about bringing up girls compared to bringing up boys.

Did you know that Venus and Uranus are the only two planets in our solar system that rotate clockwise? But Venus's rotation was actually stopped, probably by an impact, and then reversed, whereas Uranus was only knocked over on its side and continues to spin in the same direction it did when it was formed. So when author John Gray said women were from Venus—which also happens to be the hottest planet in our solar system—perhaps he was hinting that female creatures, in general, not only rotate in a different direction than male creatures, but edge more toward the emotional side.

> I learned a very important lesson: You don't talk to girls the way you talk to boys.

For instance, when I coached girls' middle school basketball, I learned a very important lesson: You don't talk to girls the way you talk to boys. If you do, they'll cry. In fact, if you surprise them and yell at them quickly, they might just run to the locker room.

That can be extremely inconvenient in the middle of a basketball game, especially when you touch the emotional hot button of your starting center. Now she's in the shower area crying her eyes out.

Worse than that, what if two of her teammates saw her run to the locker room, and they have to go and comfort her? So, in the middle of a sixty-second timeout, three of your players are in the locker room—the crier and the support team. The whistle blows, and your team is short, all because of a short conversation you had with the starting center. She had been wailing about what another girl did to her, and you simply said, "What am I? Your mother?"

Evidently it was the wrong thing to say.

I learned my lesson.

Dads, your daughters are not like you emotionally, and the faster you learn that, the better for both of you. I've been navigating my four daughters' emotions for forty-two years, as well as my wife's.

I don't know any men who say, "I love it when my daughter cries, or when my wife cries." Most men don't know what to do when the tears start flowing.

Well, men, I'm going to save you some of the crying jags and the helplessness you feel when that happens by showing you how to approach your daughter—with your manliness still intact. After all, every daughter needs a good, healthy dose of masculinity in her life, and you're the best one to convey that. The bonus is that the same principles work with the other women in your family too.

> To be the best dad to your daughter, you don't have to surrender your masculinity.

To be the best dad to your daughter, you don't have to surrender your masculinity. You don't have to watch HGTV, *Project Runway*, or the Food Network. You don't have to eat quiche or TiVo *The View*.

You can apply these principles and go on being the predictable guy you are. The man who can wear the same shirt for a couple of days with no problem. The guy who knows what he wants for breakfast four days (or four weeks) before it happens. The man whose life is complete if he's the reigning champion in his fantasy football league and his wife lets him watch ESPN. We're merely going to tweak you a bit so you can capably navigate the sometimes dangerous female waters on the home front.

Like the time when you're talking with your fifteen-year-old daughter about the cost of her dress for an upcoming gala. You're a little stressed by the $400 price tag, and you make a simple, straightforward comment. You're bamboozled by your daughter's fury in response.

She glares at you and yells, "You don't get it. You'll never get it. You'll never understand!" Then she bolts up the stairs, into her bedroom, and slams the door.

Even worse, she yells on the way, "M-o-o-om, Dad just . . ." and Mama Bear whips around the corner angrily to see what you did to Baby Cub.

In addition, Wifey gives you that "look" every married man fears more than a visit by the IRS.

Now you're in major trouble with two of the female population in your house.

Yet all you said was, "Couldn't we at least look around at some other places?" It seemed like a logical question to ask—after all, that dress costs more than your first car. So where did you go wrong?

Ah, yes, the feminine mind will take some time to get used to, Dad, but you're a smart guy. If you're forearmed with the right tools, and forewarned with the right knowledge, you'll be fine.

You already know your daughter is occasionally weird. She's that way when she's young, and she'll still be that way when she's old. To quote Mrs. Uppington, one of my pet names for my wonderful, classy bride, "The eleven-year-old female is the strangest creature on the planet." One day your daughter loves something passionately; the next day she hates it. You, Dad, have to be the steadying force.

> Whether male or female, there's something in this book for you.

Whether male or female, there's something in this book for you. But primarily, this is for dads, because deep down inside, we all want to be the best dads to our daughters that we can be.

If you're a male and not a dad yet, then

good for you that you're reading this book and doing your research early. When I was seventeen and sitting in English class, I vowed to myself, *Someday, when I figure out how to do life, I'm going to be a father . . . and a good one.* You see, being a good dad was important to me, since I didn't have much of a relationship with my father, who tipped back far too many brewskis, until later in life. But I had a very close relationship with my mom, who was a saint walking this earth. Later in this book, you'll see why the cross-gender relationships are the most important in forming a child's character and perspective on life. That's why *your relationship with your daughter* is so paramount.

I decided early on in life that I wanted to be a different kind of father with my own children. Ask any one of them, and they'll tell you I have been, as much as humanly possible. So whether you want to do early research for when you become a daddy someday, you and your wife currently have a bun in the oven and you want to be prepared, or you're already in the trenches of the daddy-daughter relationship and want to fine-tune it or get it on the right track, this book is for you.

Moms, this book is also for you. If you're married, there's nothing that makes a woman melt more than seeing her husband be a good daddy—a loving, steady, protective male figure in her daughter's life. But sometimes you don't know how to go about getting that result in your husband. Nagging doesn't work. It only shuts us men down.

That man you live with is very different from you. He thinks differently and acts differently, yet you know instinctively his role is huge in your daughter's life, and that she desperately wants to please him. But that husband you love isn't always the most sensitive person in the world, doesn't always understand your daughter, and can sometimes be too rough, harsh, or close-minded. Sometimes he even comes across like he's the king and everybody around him ought to serve him. In *Be the Dad She Needs You to Be* I'll reveal a few tricks of the trade for getting the results you long for—a husband who would take a bullet for you and one who will make a real difference in your daughter's life. We men—it's not that we don't want to try and do better; it's that we're often clueless about relationships. However, with some gentle nudging from you—the woman we value most to be in our corner—and a few attaboys for our successes, we can get headed in the right direction mighty fast. We simply need your relational wisdom to get us moving along.

If you're a single mom, you might be feeling guilty for not having that daddy influence in your daughter's life—whether part-time, full-time, or at all. There's wonderful grist for the mill in this book for you, too, for the relationships you're maneuvering through now and the ones you will be navigating in the future.

For you daughters of all ages, this book is also for you. Some of you have experienced a very close relationship with your father, and the benefits of that are revealed in your life now. Others of you are the by-products of divorce, feeling caught between Mom and Dad.

Still others of you have endured a rocky relationship with your dad, who wasn't physically or emotionally available to you. He wasn't the understanding, caring, and loving father you dreamed of. He may have been distant, hurtful, or even abusive. You might be estranged from your dad at this point—not even talking. Perhaps you couldn't tell me where he's living right now. Or you might have established a "simply tolerate each other" relationship, where you placate him, talk only on the surface of things, and avoid other topics. You don't have a deep relationship, because there are problems in your past relationship. Yet, even though you can't explain it, at your heart, you desire more than anything to have a daddy-daughter connection. That's because the daddy-daughter relationship defines who you feel you are at your heart and how valued you feel in this world. I'll walk you through the reasons for that in this book.

I've been a part of watching multitudes of daddies and daughters who were estranged from each other come together, make amends, and enjoy the time they have left on this earth. In fact, there's nothing more satisfying for a guy like me who works with people behind closed doors than to see those kinds of magical transformations take place.

They can happen for you too.

ONE

The Relationship
That Matters Most

*Why you matter, especially to your daughter,
and what's missing when you're AWOL.*

When my daughter Krissy graduated from high school, I was invited to be the main speaker. On commencement day, as I looked out over the sea of graduates with their excited faces, I said, "We've come not to celebrate your achievements, but to celebrate who you are." Then my gaze landed on my daughter . . . and I broke down and cried.

No, I'm not usually a blubbering sap. I don't often cry in public. In fact, I speak to top CEOs and governors of our nation, and have shared platforms with people such as Bill Cosby, Larry King, Amy Grant, Barbara Walters, Regis Philbin, and Franklin Graham, and I've not cried. I've even had a great time on TV shows such as *The View*, with those wild and wonderful ladies, and not cried. So what brought on the emotion that time? Because I was speaking about and to my *daughter*, and this was a big transition time in her life and in ours.

1

There's something very special about the daddy-daughter connection. You already know it, or you wouldn't be reading this book.

Why Dad Is So Important

The busiest day for every phone service in America is Mother's Day. Women are the centerpiece of the home, so we assume that mothers are the key in families. But the clout that a dad has is undeniable.

At first blush, everyone thinks the most important relationships in the family are the father-son and mother-daughter relationships. But they're wrong. The cross-gender relationships are most critical. Why does a dad matter so much to a daughter, in particular? A dad is the one who teaches a daughter what a male is all about. It's the first man in her life—the first man she loves, the first male she tries to please, the first man who says no to her, the first man to discipline her. In effect, he sets her up for success or failure with the opposite sex. Not only that, but she takes cues from how Dad treats Mom as she grows up about what to expect as a woman who is in a relationship with a man. So Dad sets up his daughter's marriage relationship too. And if that dad is a man of faith, he all of a sudden takes on the awesome responsibility of representing almighty God himself. Wow. If that made you a little nervous, then you're a smart man.

If Dad is a loving, steady, balanced man in his approach with his daughter, she will have a sense of security, love, and trust in her relationships with men. She will also stand up for herself if males attempt to take advantage of her, because she knows that her daddy would never treat her that way or allow her to be treated that way.

However, if a daughter doesn't have security, love, and trust in her relationship with her dad, that daughter will pay for the lack of those critical things all her life. She will be driven toward men who aren't good for her, who treat her badly—and she'll allow it because it's consistent with the way she views herself in relationship to men.

If Daddy treated me this way, she'll think, *then all men must be like this, so I guess I have to put up with it to have a man in my life.*

Stop for a minute and ask yourself, *Who really loved me and believed in me just the way I was when I was growing up?*

Do you have a list of twenty people? Ten? Five?

I doubt it. If you're the typical person living today, you're blessed if you have one person who believed in you and loved you unconditionally as you were growing up. If you have two people, you're doubly blessed. If you have three, call the newspaper. It's hot enough for the late-breaking news!

> Stop for a minute and ask yourself, *Who really loved me and believed in me just the way I was when I was growing up?*

This is your chance to be that kind of person for your daughter.

The Impact of AWOL Dads

Father figures are so important in the home that some girls who don't grow up with a good daddy develop what is called *father hunger.* They elaborately make up a father in their imagination, and then pretend that their dad is like that. The US Census Bureau reports that more than twenty-four million children in America don't live with their biological fathers—that's one out of every three! "Nearly 2 in 3 (64%) African American children live in father-absent homes. One in three (34%) Hispanic children, and 1 in 4 (25%) white children live in father-absent homes. . . . Children who live absent their biological fathers are, on average, at least two to three times more likely to be poor, to use drugs, to experience educational, health, emotional and behavioral problems, to be victims of child abuse, and to engage in criminal behavior than their peers who live with their married, biological (or adoptive) parents."[1]

The National Fatherhood Initiative reports the devastating effects of father absence:

- *They experience poverty.* Children in homes without fathers are "almost four times more likely to be poor."
- *They struggle with emotional and behavior problems.* "Children born to single mothers show higher levels of aggressive behavior than children born to married mothers. Living in a single-mother household is equivalent to experiencing 5.25 partnership transitions."
- *They turn to crime.* "Youths . . . had significantly higher odds of incarceration than those in mother-father families." Interestingly, minority adolescents who were ages ten to fourteen who had "frequent communication with nonresident biological fathers decreased adolescent delinquency."
- *They experiment with sexual activity and experience teen pregnancy.* "Being raised by a single mother raises the risk of teen pregnancy, marrying with less than a high school degree, and forming a marriage where both partners have less than a high school degree."[2]

In addition, St. Louis's Fathers' Support Center says that 70 percent of African-American children live in households with no father.

> [Founder Halbert Sullivan] understands absent fathers on a deeply personal level. He used to be one.
>
> Addicted to drugs since 1965, Sullivan was a self-professed "deadbeat dad" until his children were 10 and 18.
>
> "I was no good for 27 or 28 years." [Finally, depressed and desperate, he went to a rehab facility, earned two graduate degrees, and started working with kids in local high schools.] Those efforts led to his being asked to lead an institution to help fathers.
>
> Since 1998, the Fathers' Support Center has served 8,800 men of all races but mostly African American, and their families. Seventy-five percent of those who graduate from the program now support their children.[3]

I see real-life proof of father absence, whether emotional or physical, all the time in the women who attend my seminars. Jennifer was in her late thirties when I met her. She said she'd had a really bad marriage and was now divorced, a single mom. When I asked her to describe her father, she paused, and then said, "Well, he wasn't around much, and when he was, he was really messed up."

"So let me make a guess about your ex-husband. He was exactly like your father, right?"

She winced. "Yes."

Because Jennifer suffered from DADD—Daddy Attention Deficit Disorder—she had spent her life looking for a daddy's affirmation, acceptance, and presence. Forced to prove her worth by taking care of others, she ended up marrying a man who was an alcoholic and a loser.

The Benefits of an Engaged Dad

When daughters have engaged dads, they benefit from that relationship for a lifetime. Here are a few of the benefits:

- *They have higher self-worth.* Girls who have the secure love of a father see themselves in a more positive light. They are able to stand up for themselves and make good decisions.
- *They rebel less, especially in the critical years.* A dad who rules with an iron fist and demands respect only increases a daughter's desire to rebel against the rules. Dads who relate to their daughters in a respectful manner earn their respect. Daughters with dads who are involved in their lives will tend to be less involved with drugs and crime because they don't need to look outside the home for love and acceptance. They also will say no more easily in dating situations and have a lower possibility of becoming pregnant outside of marriage. If you go down to the local prison and talk to the inmates, you'd find few who had actively, positively engaged fathers.
- *Their adult relationships are healthier.* The way Dad treats them is the way they expect others to treat them. Does your family get the leftovers of your time—after golf, after the football game is over, after the car gets fixed,

after you finish an extra project for work? Then that's what your daughter will expect out of her own husband later. Don't miss out on some of the most influential work you can ever do.

- *Their life trajectories are more successful.* When a dad believes in a daughter, she feels she can do anything. She won't put up with guff from others, and she'll power ahead through difficult situations because she knows her dad loves her and believes in her.

Dads, I know you love your daughters deeply, or you wouldn't be taking the time to read this book. One day, that girl of yours will take everything you have given her—or haven't given her—and step out into the world. Her marital satisfaction, her ability to parent her children and relate in particular to any sons she might have, and her sense of well-being and acceptance will be something that she has achieved in spite of or, in part, because of you.

If you have a negative legacy from your own father, or if your wife has one from her father, it's time to stop the cycle. Your daughter deserves your absolute best.

Some of you reading this book are daughters. Your growing-up experiences represent all kinds of dads—actively engaged and loving dads; emotionally missing dads; verbally, physically, or emotionally abusive dads; divorced dads living other places; or completely absent dads. You, of all people, know the impact fathers can have on their daughters' lives because you are living proof, whether you realized it or not until this moment. Don't hesitate to share that perspective with the men in your life. They need to know that what they do in the home matters—that *they* matter—for a daughter's lifetime.

What I Remember About Dad . . .

It's the little things that count in the long run, daughters say:

"He laughed with me when I blew dandelion fluff for the first time."

"We played Frisbee every Saturday morning in the summer."

"He held me when my first boyfriend dumped me, and I cried."

"Fall is still my favorite time of year. When I was young, Dad and I lined up plastic lawn chairs to form a tunnel and dumped a long line of leaves over them in the fall to make a leaf fort. Dad even crawled through it right behind me. He always made hot chocolate when we were done."

"He played a computer game with me and told my older brothers they had to play outside."

"He always muted the TV remote when I asked him a question."

"I heard him telling a coworker how proud he was of me for having such a giving heart."

"He let me take his shoes off every day when he got home from work."

"We didn't have a lot of money, but my dad lavished his time and attention on me. That was way better than stuff."

"He still kisses my mom, even though they've been married, like, forever."

The Moments You'll Think About . . . for the Rest of Your Life

Some of you may be like me—actively working at being an engaged dad. Most of the time you do well, but every once in a while your priorities slip. I want to tell you about one slip of mine and what I learned as a result.

Our firstborn daughter, Holly, was in her senior year of college when she was chosen as a finalist for homecoming queen. I was on the road, giving a parenting seminar that had been scheduled long before we knew that she was even a queen candidate. Once I knew she'd been chosen as a finalist, I told my co-speaker for the seminar, "Hey, I need to leave the seminar early. My daughter's running for queen and there's a big to-do—a parade, homecoming game, the dance. I simply can't miss it."

My co-speaker understood how I felt, but since several hundred people had already signed up for the seminar, which was to include both of us for both days, he asked, "How can I tell them you'll only be here for part of it?"

So, rather than following my daddy instinct, I stood behind my former commitment.

When Holly was elected homecoming queen, I was not there to share that special event with her. To this day, I wish I had said, "I am leaving anyway."

But I didn't.

Because of the remorse I've felt ever since then, I now go out of my way to put my family first . . . in everything. Lesson learned the hard way.

You might have experienced one or more of the same type of slips. Like me, you can't change the past. But you can certainly change the present and the future so that your daddy's heart aligns with your life priorities.

Your Worth as a Man

I was forty-four, and my wife, Sande, was forty-two. We had three kids—two girls and a boy. Our youngest was nine years old. My career was taking off, our finances were comfortable, and life felt perfect. At last I could relax and enjoy my family and more of life.

But God Almighty had something different in mind. Sande and I were enjoying a steak dinner when she slipped me a home-made card with the words *Are you ready to change your vacation? Are you ready to change your sleeping habits?*

Huh, I thought. *Am I missing a joke?*

"Turn it over," my lovely wife suggested with sparkling eyes.

I did, and it simply said, *Merry Christmas.* But the picture caught my eye—Santa Claus was holding a cute little baby with a toothless grin. My jaw dropped. "Does this mean what I think it means?"

Enter daughter number three, Hannah.

Five years later, once again thinking our family was complete, forty-seven-year-old Sande surprised me again. This time, at age forty-nine, I was even less charitable. I wanted to kill something. After all, I quickly did the math. When my baby grew up and entered high school, I'd probably be drooling over my walker during the PTA meeting.

> I quickly did the math. When my baby grew up and entered high school, I'd probably be drooling over my walker during the PTA meeting.

Yet, if you asked our youngest, Lauren, to complete the sentence, "You are Daddy's ...," ten-to-one she'd say, "gift from God."

Yes, our lives were disrupted twice

when we thought our family was complete. However, who those girls have become since then confirms to me continually that, no matter what I do for my career, I'll never be more fulfilled than I am as the father of four daughters and one son.

Fast-forward a few years, to when Hannah and Lauren were in elementary school. When I walked through the front door, it didn't matter what they were doing—eating an ice cream sundae, playing with a favorite friend—they'd drop what they were doing and make a beeline for me.

Isn't that an amazing feeling, Dad, when your girl is keyed in to the arrival of her father and can't wait to hug you? Enjoy those moments . . . every single one of them.

My young daughters didn't care how much money I'd made that day. They couldn't care less how many books I sold, or whether two dozen or two thousand people showed up to hear me speak. The doctoral degree behind my name meant nothing to them. I could have been a high school dropout (which I very nearly was), and they'd have felt the same way. I was their *dad*, and no one could take my place.

No one can take your place either. Your company can replace you (and they eventually will), but in your daughter's eyes there will always be only one of you. So why expend all your energy outside your home for what won't matter in the long run? I know you often feel caught in the middle; I was. At the time when most men are starting a family, they're also climbing a couple of rungs on the corporate ladder. The time they're most needed at home is when they're pulled most strongly toward work.

But what's really most important in the long run? Of all the things you do in life, what will make you matter most? Do your kids and wife really need another ten thousand dollars a year? By the time you subtract Uncle Sam's donation from that, you've got a lot less anyway. Or would they benefit more from a dad who makes it home in time for dinner?

What your family needs most is simple: you.

A Good Dad's Quick Reference Guide

- Engage in your daughter's life to stay in her heart.
- Be loving, steady, and balanced.

TWO

Dads Do It ~~Better~~ Different

*It might not be what Mom would do, but you, Dad,
can still get the job done . . . and done well.*

Back in the day when there wasn't such a thing as Pampers but only the cloth variety of diapers, I was home alone with our firstborn, Holly, who was eighteen months old, and Krissy, our second born, an infant. Well, that day, Holly had the worst big-ba since Franco American spaghetti was created. Truly. It was unbelievable. I didn't have a clue what to do. It was literally running down her legs onto the kitchen floor.

I didn't have time to put on my "What Would Mommy Do?" bracelet. This was survival.

So what did this dad do? I grabbed Holly, yanked the screen door of the kitchen open, and bolted into the backyard. At that point, I really didn't care what the neighbors thought. I was on a targeted mission. That day the garden hose saved my life . . . and the kitchen from an even more aromatic disaster.

The best part is, I got away with it . . . for three days. Then little bigmouth Holly started talking to her mother about the "special shower"—that's what she called it—Daddy gave her.

13

My wife lifted an imperious eyebrow. "What special shower?" she asked.

"In the backyard with the hose," Holly announced. "And it was cold."

Mrs. Uppington gave me "the Look," followed with, "Leemie, what did you do?"

"Hey," I defended myself, "I didn't know what to do. It was an unbelievable mess." At her further icy stare, I added, "And I swabbed the kitchen floor, too, so don't give me the Look."

We dads may not do the job the way moms would, but we get the job done.

Even if it means we have to do things our way, with the garden hose.

Gender Differences 101

Clearly, daddies do things differently than mommies.

I've never had the compulsion to ask a waiter, "Excuse me, what does that man have on his plate over there?" then follow it with, "Oooh, it looks good. I'd like to try that."

I also have no interest in getting my hair done once a week, like my beloved wife, or even once a month. I just put my baseball hat on. It goes nicely with the same T-shirt I had on yesterday and the same shorts I wore yesterday. They all have that "broken in" feel to them.

> Clearly, daddies do things differently than mommies.

We dads use a lot fewer words than moms. In fact, we're known for our grunts, which can carry an entire conversation in their tone.

And we do stupid things, even at ages where we should know better. My wife says that my lifelong best buddy, Moonhead, and I act like two otters playing in the stream whenever we see each other. We'll go into a restaurant and say, "Well, what are you going to have, fat boy?"

"What are you going to have, larger than most?"

We've also been known to wrestle each other in public. And we're in our sixties. Not much has changed since we were young boys in Upstate New York, other than the fact that we now have wives who roll their eyes at our antics.

At a young age, males and females are different.

Young girls of ages three, four, and five are already using "we" talk—very inclusive and relationally oriented. Young boys of the same age use "I" or "me" talk—very exclusive.

Girls walk hand in hand out of a gymnasium. They give a little skip and hop, laugh, talk, and share. The boys? They're in single file. They've got that lope kind of gait, and they're lookin' cool. They even walk a little slower the world over.

Girls talk and negotiate with each other, participating in groupthink. For boys, competition and doing it solo is in their very nature. They're constantly trying to outdo each other at anything . . . and everything.

Watch boys and girls play sometime if you want a chuckle.

> What Boys Do: Wrestle and flex their muscles.
> What Girls Do: Hold hands and share.

The other day I was at a mall in Tucson, Arizona, with my wife. I try my best to avoid such places, but sometimes, being the good husband that I am, I get cajoled into going so I can "share" the experience with my wife. Since my wife had some major shopping on the brain, I told her I'd meet her back in the food court. Right next to the food is this wonderful little playground. So I sat and watched the kids for entertainment.

Two little girls were playing nicely together, negotiating what they were going to do next, discussing the possibilities.

Then I looked at the two boys. One had a balloon and was beating his friend over the head with it as fast and hard as he could.

Is one better than the other?

No, they're simply different.

I'm in the counseling profession. Last week I stood before an audience of three thousand people and asked them, "How many of you women would like to go to counseling this week?"

There was a sea of hands.

"Oh, Dr. Leman, I'd love to go," one woman called.

"Yeah," called another. "I'd even get a new outfit and get my hair done for the occasion."

Then I asked the men in the audience. No hands.

Frankly, there's not a man who's sane who would put his hand up.

The male thinking goes like this (if you're a female reading this book, say it out loud with the tone of Rocky Balboa, the fighter from the *Rocky* movies, and you'll have the most vivid picture): *Why would I tell a stranger what's going on in my life? Especially a shrink kind of guy. There's no way I'm telling anybody anything. And I'm certainly not paying somebody big money to hear my problems. I'll deal with my problems myself.*

> We men are driven to compete, not to show weakness by airing our dirty laundry in public.

We men are driven to compete, not to show weakness by airing our dirty laundry in public.

We men also work hard at handling one thing at a time. Women are multitaskers and, frankly, a little intimidating to us men.

Especially when we aren't always as observant as we most likely should be.

Case in point: about six months ago, Mrs. Uppington gave me a new toothbrush. An Oral-B toothbrush. It seemed to be sort of fat and heavy for a toothbrush, but I didn't really think much about it. I simply threw out the old one and stashed the new one in my travel bag.

After taking a flight back after a speaking engagement, I headed to the parking lot at the airport, found my car, and started it up. As I drove toward home, I kept hearing a noise.

I thought something was wrong with the car. I even pulled off the side of the road and turned off the car so I could listen. The noise continued. Opening the hood, I peered around to see if some part was still engaged. But everything looked normal.

I slammed the hood down and proceeded to drive home. I had to stop at Krissy's house to drop something off.

My grandson, Conner, was nine years old at the time. I pulled into Krissy's driveway and turned off the car.

Conner came running. "Hi, Grampy!"

"Conner," I said, "can you help Grampy?"

"Sure, Grampy," he answered, all smiles and always ready to solve a problem. "What do you want?"

"Come on over here and listen to my car. Can you hear that noise?"

"Sure, Grampy."

"Where is it coming from?"

Conner cocked his head and then pointed. "It's in your suitcase."

My suitcase was stashed on the passenger front seat of the convertible. I opened it up and looked inside. My toiletry bag was vibrating. I unzipped it, and inside was my toothbrush, buzzing against my aftershave bottle like a mini-jackhammer pounding away.

As God is my judge, I noticed for the first time—I'd been brushing my teeth with the thing for at least ninety days—that there were two little buttons on the toothbrush. I laughed so hard at myself.

We men might not notice the little things.

We may never be able to find things in the fridge that women can.

The other day I asked Sande, "Honey, where's the mustard?"

"It's on the right side, on the second shelf," she called.

I looked again. "I'm telling you, it's not here," I called back.

Sande sashayed into the kitchen with that "Look" on her face. The one that says, kindly of course, *I think I married an idiot.*

With a grand flourish, she reached past me, to the right side, on the second shelf, moved one item, and sure enough, there was the mustard.

Okay, so sometimes I am an idiot, without sonar.

But I care deeply about my family.

I'm not my wife. I can't always find the mustard. I don't wear a skirt. I don't have the legs for it.

I'm all male.

And that's okay by me.

How Men Juggle Apples

One at a time

How Women Juggle Apples

Three to five at a time

What We Men Are Really Good At

When one of my daughters was fourteen, I took her on a flight to New York City with me. I was booked to do a national TV show, and I wanted her to see behind the scenes of what I did for a living. We had a great time together. Then, when I had to tape another show, I arranged to have the car drive us by Bloomingdale's on the way and drop her off, since she loved to shop. I told her I'd meet her back in the restaurant at Bloomingdale's at a certain time.

At the appointed time, I asked the car to drop me off at Bloomingdale's and wait for me while I ran in to the restaurant to pick up my daughter.

She wasn't there. A few minutes went by, and I got nervous. My daughter was always responsible and punctual. A half hour later she wasn't there, and I started freaking out. I hoofed it to the office to put out an all-points bulletin on my daughter . . . and found out there were *five* different restaurants in Bloomingdale's.

Houston, we have a problem, I thought. So I did what all men do in a crisis. I called my wife back in Tucson, Arizona.

"Hi, honey, are you guys having a good time?" she said excitedly.

"Yeah . . ."

> I did what all men do in a crisis. I called my wife.

My wife's a smart cookie. She knew right away by my tone something was up. "Leemie, what have you done?"

"Actually, honey, I can't find her."

There was a pause, then, "What did you say?"

"Now don't get upset," I began.

"I'm not upset," my wife said in a frosty tone. "But tell me what I think I heard you say."

"I'm sure I'll find her," I explained. "There aren't that many people in New York City."

Let's just say my attempt at humor fell flat, and my normally calm wife went ballistic on the phone. For my part, I was more frantic than she was. I thought my daughter had been abducted.

The general manager's office paged her and . . . nothing.

Another page . . . same thing.

Long story short, my daughter was waiting in the restaurant for me. When I didn't show up, she began to look for me, while I looked for her. She, too, found out about the multiple restaurants, so she started walking to each different one. We were like two ships passing in the night. (And that, parents, is why your daughter having a cell phone when she's away from you is so important. My daughter didn't have one at that point.)

Finally we reunited two hours later, but in the meantime, the car driver got tired of waiting for me and took off with my luggage in the car. I didn't have his phone number; he didn't have mine. Needless to say, we missed our plane. It was a real mess.

Now, if it had been Mrs. Uppington with our daughter in New York City at Bloomingdale's, she would have gotten out of that car, walked our daughter into the store, stood in the restaurant, and stated, "See this X right here? I'll meet you right here at this exact spot at 4:00 p.m."

Me? I merely said, "I'll meet you in the restaurant, honey. You have a good time."

You see why we men need you women?

So men aren't always good at the details or with specifics, but we are good at many things. Sadly, today's society doesn't seem to have much use for men. In fact, if you watch sitcoms, which bash men with great regularity, you get the distinct impression that men aren't needed for anything. But if you don't think men are needed in the family, take a look again at the stats I shared in chapter 1 about what happens when dads are emotionally or physically AWOL. Every bit of research shows that your daughter will do better in life because you're there. We men don't do things the same way, but male role models are needed to balance that wonderful female creature called a woman.

We Are, at Our Core, Difference Makers

The reality is that the huge majority of us dads want to make a difference in our kids' lives. We want to be of service to other people. We want to be great dads and husbands. But we don't always have the tools we need to do that.

Rest assured, Dad, that you are the biggest difference maker in your daughter's life. The attention you give her, the affirmation you shower upon her, the approval you provide her—all gets internalized by your daughter to the point where she adopts the internal perspective: *I am somebody. I'm a (your last name). I'm a worthwhile human being. I don't have to take ill treatment from anyone. And I won't.*

We Are Problem Solvers

To see men shine, give us a problem and we'll go after it until it's solved. We're relentless. We want to provide answers, be the family "go-to" guy. Solving problems helps fulfill our three greatest needs—to be wanted, respected, and fulfilled—as a part of the family.

For example, my lovely wife is a sleeper. She truly has raccoon-like qualities. The woman can sleep anytime—even on a bench at a ball game (yes, it used to be embarrassing, but by now my best buddy, Moonhead, is used to it). She stays up very late and then sleeps until late in the morning. Her idea of getting an early start is two o'clock in the afternoon. Some of our daughters inherited those qualities from their mother. Me? I'm up at the crack of dawn and have completed half my day before she's even up.

> To see men shine, give us a problem.

When our kids were little, Mrs. Uppington definitely needed to sleep. But our kids could be up at the crack of dawn, and keeping little ones quiet was a task that even Superman couldn't accomplish. So I solved the problem for her every Saturday, even without her asking. I'd load Holly and Krissy in the car—still barefoot in their Pooh Bear nighties—and take them to Dunkin' Donuts. They loved to sit on the swivel stools. They'd twirl and twirl while they ate their doughnuts and drank their milk. We'd spend a couple hours every Saturday morning away from the house so Mrs. Raccoon could sleep.

Looking back now, I realize that Mrs. Uppington would have been aghast at the thought of her kids out in public without shoes on (all those germs on the floor, you know) and still in their jammies (socially unacceptable). But it didn't bother them, and it didn't bother me. In fact, we probably gave a few Dunkin' Donuts visitors some chuckles. And when we went home, Sande was ready with recharged energy and smiles for all of us. Problem solved! It worked for all of us. What Sande didn't know didn't hurt her either.

As soon as Sande got pregnant with Holly, our oldest, she had made a firm decision that she was going to stay home and rear our kids. When all the kids were older, though, and in school, Sande went on to launch her own retail store, the Shabby Hattie Antique Shop, and enjoyed the benefits and satisfaction of owning a business. No more was I taking little kids to Dunkin' Donuts on Saturday. Instead, I cooked dinner on the nights she worked late at the shop.

Now, my dinners didn't look anything like hers. In fact, they were rather long, spaced-out affairs, with one food item served at a time.

"Hey, kids," I'd call, "the corn is ready."

Twenty minutes later, I'd say, "Pork chops are ready," and there was another race to the table.

I didn't worry about the four food groups or that every color was represented on the table. I didn't even set the table with the fork on the left side and the knife and spoon on the right. But I fed our family's bellies. I got the job done, the problem solved.

Dad, when you walk in your wife's shoes, you discover some realities you might otherwise miss. Children have no timetables. Their needs are often immediate. They have patience as thin as waxed paper. And being around young kids all day will tax your patience, too, as much as you love them.

Your wife isn't the only one who needs your help in solving problems. Your daughter does too. She needs you to anticipate her needs before she has them—and before they become the size of Mount Vesuvius. She needs you to help her look at situations logically and from multiple angles, rather than from the one lens she may be looking through, colored with emotions. But she doesn't need you to handle every situation for her. Every child needs to learn how to solve her own problems. However, in order for daughters to do that with confidence, they need a dad's listening ear as they process.

We Are Calculated Risk Takers

Contrast the way moms and dads treat their kids when teaching them how to swim.

Take Mom first. She's most likely to let her young child float in an inner tube in a calm, serene way, pushing the child inch by inch away from the side of the pool. In fact, if Mom could find a way to teach her daughter to swim without getting wet, she would.

Now, listen for the screams. Chances are, you'll find a daddy behind them. All of a sudden that daughter has become a projectile missile, thrown out of her daddy's arms, up into the air, and into the water with a dramatic *sploosh*, then caught up again. And the next daughter is already shouting, "Now do it to me, Daddy! I'm next!"

How does Mom respond? She says in a panic, "Uh, dear, do you think that's safe? They really don't know how to swim!"

"Don't worry, honey. Kids at this age are really flexible. Throwing them in the water is the best way for them to learn how to swim."

> So Mama Duck sits on the side and clucks away in worry, while Papa Duck gets those ducklings paddling in the water.

So Mama Duck sits on the side and clucks away in worry, while Papa Duck gets those ducklings paddling in the water.

Dad, the way you play with your kids and encourage them to take on life is usually completely different from the way your wife does. You bring certain testosterone-laden qualities and characteristics to your relationship with your kids that are necessary for your daughter to achieve a balanced perspective about life.

So go on taking those calculated risks that might make your wife squeamish at times, like having your child jump from her two-story playhouse into your arms. It will build in your daughter not only the ability to take risks, but a trust in you that will last for a lifetime.

We Are Defenders, Protectors

On September 11, 2001, I stared at the television, watching the brave firemen as they ran into burning, disintegrating buildings to rescue the survivors of the most vicious attack on domestic soil that America has ever experienced. Choking back tears, I said to Sande, "Look at those guys. Now those are real men."

Real men are difference makers who want to help those in crisis. They are the defenders, the protectors of the family and those who are less fortunate.

One summer our nine-year-old daughter, Hannah, needed to fly from our summer home in New York State to Tucson, Arizona, where we spend the school year. I didn't want her to fly alone, so I accompanied her. I reserved a round-trip ticket that had me flying back to Buffalo forty-five minutes after Hannah and I arrived in Tucson, and I dropped her off at her friend's house so they could enjoy time together before school started.

When the flight attendant found out what I was doing— spending an entire day flying from Buffalo to Tucson and then immediately back to Buffalo, solely to chaperone my daughter, she couldn't believe it. "For fifty bucks, you could have saved yourself a whole lot of trouble. Why don't you just put her on the plane? We chaperone kids much younger than her all the time. Don't you trust us? We do a good job."

I looked that flight attendant right in the eye and said, "It's not your job. It's mine."

Her jaw dropped. She literally didn't know what to say. Before the flight was over, several attendants had gathered around to talk to the crazy man who insisted on flying with his daughter.

Today not only do men have to be the physical protectors of our daughters, we also need to be the emotional protectors. Here's what I mean.

I can't tell you how many times I've witnessed this type of scene over the years:

A young woman walks into the room, where a group of women are standing.

"Oh, your necklace is adorable," one tells her.

"And your hairdo . . . I love it. It's perfect for the summer," another says.

"Where did you get that outfit, and those shoes? I have to know," the third one adds.

As soon as the young woman walks out of the room, the group of women closes back in and starts throwing barbs at her:

"Can you believe that hideous outfit?"

"And those shoes—where on earth did she find those?"

"Her haircut looks like somebody put a bowl around her head . . ."

Females can be vicious in their rhetoric with each other. That's why, Dad, you're in a very good position to explain to your daughter why she should be careful what she says in person.

But what your daughter puts in print is also critically important. She might think the Internet, instant messaging, and texting are only between her and her girlfriend, but as soon as her girlfriend hits the forward button, only God himself knows where the information might end up, including in the computer of the one person in this world she'd hate to have that e-mail.

When my mom dragged me to Sunday school, we sang a

children's song that includes the lyrics, "O be careful little eyes what you see . . . O be careful little ears what you hear."[1] As archaic as those words sound, they're great advice for all young people today. If you don't share that with her, who will? Or will you let her learn that lesson the hard way?

My Knight on the Roller-Skating Rink

My dad's pretty even tempered, and he's always been very involved in my life. When I was thirteen, he took me and a group of my friends to a roller-skating rink. A guy there who wasn't part of our group kept skating around me, knocking me down. The second time it happened, my dad stepped into the rink and was by my side to help me up. He steered me to the side of the rink, then headed for the guy who knocked me down, grabbed his arm, and got right in his face. To this day I have no idea what my dad said, and he never would tell me, but that guy looked a little pasty white and hurriedly left the rink. I didn't see him the rest of the night.

Later, my dad told me, "I couldn't stand how that guy was treating you. I didn't want you to get hurt."

My dad had always watched out for me, but that night I realized, perhaps for the first time, what a protector he was—not only of me, but of my mom too. I knew I'd always be safe with my daddy.

To this day, even though I'm thirty-two, married, and have two kids of my own, I still feel that way around him and around my husband, who is a lot like my dad.

—Kendra, North Carolina

Let Your Woman Be a Woman

When people come to our home, my wife serves us all an incredible dinner. I'm talking *incredible*. She spends days thinking about the perfect menu, gathering the ingredients, and making sure the setting is beautiful. I think it's nuts, and it's one of the reasons I affectionately call her Mrs. Uppington.

However, I've realized over all our years of marriage that, if doing so is important to her, it had better be important to me. Yesterday we had a couple here—people I know but whom Sande had never met. I told her a few days before that the couple was coming for a nice, comfy, little informal lunch, and that they were going to bring an ice chest of food so they could go out in the boat and go fishing. What did Mrs. Uppington do? She planned an elaborate menu with enough classy food to feed the entire block, including these appetizer thingies in individual crystal cups and homemade strawberry ice cream pie. She also set the table with clear water glasses that have to be, as God is my judge, fourteen inches high. They reek of formality. They look like they're custom built for giraffes. I had to laugh. To my beloved bride, that was an *informal* lunch.

But the female visitor loved it all. She raved about the presentation.

I couldn't help myself. I said to the group, "Well, how do you like the tall water glasses?"

"I love them," the female visitor gushed.

I chuckled. "That's great. They're just not my favorites."

But my wife had the last laugh. "Honey, look at your water glass."

I did. She'd placed a very small water glass by my plate. It was the only one like it on the table. Everybody else had the tall giraffe glasses.

Lesson learned.

Gentlemen, let your lady be a lady. The "fussiness" you see about details is what makes her who she is . . . and is part of the mystique that made you fall in love with her in the first place.

So go ahead and be a man. Burp . . . but not in a female's presence. Do your nails at the red light with your teeth.

Just expect that, in the midst of your manliness, you'll have a few tall giraffe glasses from the females in your life.

A Good Dad's Quick Reference Guide

- Your girl isn't a boy.
- Your job: serve, protect, defend, take calculated risks, and problem-solve.

THREE

Know Your Duckling

*Why it's important for Papa Duck to know
each young'un in the flock individually.*

I'm an old grizzled veteran. I've purchased more than one
training bra, even when there was nothing to train. I've made
the runs to Walgreens for more than a few Light Days, Every
Days, Windy Days, and Almost There Days. I've looked out my
front window and seen one of my daughters standing at the side
of a car, kissing a boy—a boy I didn't even know. That certainly
caused me some deep thought. I've heard my daughters scream at
each other, "You're not wearing my sweater or my skirt. You wore
my shirt last week, and it came back dirty!"

I've gone through the battles. One of the most important
things I've learned is how important it is to get to know each girl
individually.

The Leman Ducklings

At our summer home in New York, families of ducks waddle
up onto our lawn in groups—sometimes nine, other times four,

five, or six, and sometimes only Papa Duck, Mama Duck, and one duckling. Yet when our lawn is swarmed by hordes of ducks, which all look alike to me, those mama and papa ducks know their ducklings from the others. Papa Duck proudly leads his flock across the yard to the pond, with Mama Duck at the tail end, herding the most slow moving of their ducklings along so nobody gets left behind.

Sande and I have five ducklings—four of them female. Though all are Lemans through and through, none is like the other. The trick for me as a dad is to discover each of their individual quirks and to keep them in mind as I relate to them.

Here's what I mean.

Holly

Holly, our firstborn, was the lab rat of the family. Sande and I admit it. We practiced on her. In fact, we overdid everything with her. After all, Sande had miscarried twice before she got pregnant with Holly, which meant she was even more special and long awaited than many first babies. We tiptoed around Holly and tried to keep the house quiet when she was sleeping, because she was a real piece of work. If we had to go somewhere, and that meant waking Holly up, Sande's and my conversation went something like this:

"Honey, we've got to go. You wake Holly up."

"No, I'm not waking her up. I woke her up yesterday. It's your turn."

> Holly woke up swinging.

"But . . ."

You see, Holly woke up swinging. She had this blankie with a knot in it that looked like someone had taken a machete to it. It was always tucked under her arm like a football. But when you had to wake her up, she woke up hard—and you'd better duck.

I learned as a dad that you don't talk to Holly in the morning; you simply wait until she comes around and is fully awake. Yet that same daughter today is a principal and an English teacher by trade; has great patience; is married to Dean, a wonderful man; and has all of my wife's graces. But you don't talk to her in the morning, since she has her mother's raccoonlike qualities.

Holly could read at two years old. Really, she could. When my older brother visited us when Holly was two and a half, he saw her "reading" and said to me, "She's not reading. She's memorized that book."

Holly overheard, looked up at her Uncle Jack, and spelled, "E-X-I-T, Uncle Jack." Yes, indeed, she had a great command of the English language, and she didn't hesitate to use it for her purposes.

Case in point, at the age of four, Holly told me she had decided to drop out of preschool, which with new management had changed from a warm, fuzzy experience into an experimental learning center.

"Well," I said, "if you're not going to preschool anymore, you have to call them and tell them."

"But I don't have their number," my firstborn said.

I decided to call her bluff. "Here's the number."

Holly one-upped me. She actually dialed it and told the person who answered, "This is Schlolly Leman" (she couldn't pronounce *Holly*) "and I'm not coming to school there anymore."

She never went back.

Some years later, I did an autograph party at a bookstore. Holly wanted to go with me. She asked me on the way over if she could get a book. "Sure," I said. I'd never turn down any of my kids who want to read a book.

We left the store, though, without getting her a book. I realized it an hour later and apologized to Holly.

"Don't worry, Dad," she said. "I read it."

She'd read the entire book while we were at the store.

When we went for our first appointment with Holly's kindergarten teacher, the teacher reported that Holly was doing well and adjusting to kindergarten, and that she knew everything she had to know and then some. The teacher said Holly had an affinity for words and was very discerning. One day, the teacher was trying to explain to the kids how rain was made. So he took some ice cubes and held them until the warmth of his hands made them drip. "This is rain," he said.

"Mr. Wortman," Holly said, "that's not rain. That's ice cube water."

Ah, yes.

Holly is the same child who would ask, "What time are we going to leave, Dad?"

"About ten o'clock," I'd say.

"Dad, what time specifically are we going to leave?" she'd ask.

"We'll leave at 10:10," I'd say.

"Thanks, Dad," she'd say.

She had a need to know details. She would study a problem from all angles.

That's a firstborn for you.

Firstborns are groomed for success, for leadership, and for recognition. They'll not only get a job done; they'll get it done right. Because it's usually a few years before siblings arrive, firstborns dominate the scene at home for a while. Their role models are adults—their parents.

Because we parents react to every cry right away, make a big deal about what the firstborn does, and plan every detail of our baby's day, is it any wonder that later in life your firstborn daughter will expect immediate attention, react like everything is a big deal, and have an intense need to know exactly what you're doing for the day?

Firstborns are the planners, organizers, list makers, managers, and perfectionists of the world. School is often their proving ground. They tend to be confident and self-assured in most situations. They keep things under control, set goals and reach them, and tend to get more done in a day than children who fall elsewhere in the birth order. They're great problem solvers.

> Firstborns are groomed for success, for leadership, and for recognition. They'll not only get a job done; they'll get it done right.

But the very things that make them successes can also cause problems in their relationships. Others may see them as self-centered and difficult to work with (firstborns know how things should work and expect everybody else to agree). They're sometimes afraid to try new things because they're not sure they'll succeed, and they're critical of themselves and others. They're never satisfied with the job they've done. "I could have done that better," they tell themselves. They live by the rules and aren't naturally flexible—order is very important to them. They also put themselves and others under a lot of stress and pressure and tend to be serious, failing to see the humor in situations.

Does this put some things about your firstborn in perspective, Dad? Do you see now why it's so important for you to lighten up on that already heavily burdened firstborn?

Krissy

Contrast that with Krissy, our second born, who was happy to come along for the ride. She didn't need to know the specifics of anything. She'd jump in with both feet and ask questions later.

When Krissy was seven, and we were in California, she broke

her arm. While at the hospital, the physician did what physicians are prone to do when difficult things need to be done with children. They said it was time for the parents to leave. In many cases, that's good judgment, because parents can sometimes prove to be more difficult than the wounded child. However, with Krissy, it wasn't the best judgment.

Mama Bear Sande, knowing her little cub, said, "Doctor, I don't think that's a good idea."

But he insisted . . . and got a surprise that he probably hadn't seen before, in all his years of being a physician.

You see, if Krissy finds herself in a corner, she adopts badger-like qualities—the vicious type with the steel gloves. When Krissy realized she was going to get a shot and her mother wouldn't be there, she went absolutely ballistic. So much so that, indeed, Sande was ushered back in the room to be there when Krissy got the shot.

> If Krissy finds herself in a corner, she adopts badgerlike qualities.

Though Krissy is normally sweet and easygoing—she's a kindergarten teacher now—you never, ever back her into a corner. You always have to give her an out. I learned that the hard way more than once.

For example, Krissy applied to only one college: North Park University in Chicago. It shouldn't have surprised me that a middle-born would place all her eggs in one basket, but it still made me nervous. Especially when North Park had had the good sense to kick me out as a student (though years later, they actually gave me the distinguished alumnus award).

I knew the campus well, but I still looked at it differently on move-in day when I realized the school would now house my daughter. We did all the regular things you do when you take a kid to college—meet the staff, haul suitcases and boxes to the dorm room, and meet the roommate.

At night there was an orientation dinner, where students and their parents met the president of the university. As Sande, Krissy, and I inched our way toward the front of the long line, we were seven places away from shaking the president's hand when Krissy turned to me and said, "I need to talk to you."

I lifted an eyebrow. "Now? The president is right there. We've been waiting in line—"

Her chin firmed in determination. "I need to talk to you right now."

I backed down. My badgerlike daughter was in full swing. "All right, come over here."

We stepped out of line, but Sande held our place. Any hope that this would be a short conversation was immediately dispelled when I saw the tears well in Krissy's eyes.

"I don't want to go to school here," she said.

It took a second to form any words. Then I managed to sputter, "What?"

Keep in mind, this was the only school Krissy had applied to, and it was late August. She had no other options. Even so, she insisted, "I don't want to go to school here."

"Krissy," I said, "get back in line."

"Daddy, I'm scared. I don't feel safe here. Please don't make me stay. I want to go home with you and Mom."

Earlier in the day, some yahoo driving a truck had scared Krissy half to death when he raced through an alley at about forty miles per hour, barely missing her as she dodged the vehicle.

Few words get a father's attention more than "I don't feel safe here." But I knew this wasn't the time to make a snap decision.

"Listen," I said, "we're going to shake the president's hand.

> Few words get a father's attention more than "I don't feel safe here."

See your mother? She's almost at the front. And then we're going to sit down and enjoy this chicken dinner together as a family. We'll talk more after that."

Crestfallen, Krissy slipped back in line. Needless to say, it was a very long dinner. Krissy didn't eat a thing. She didn't even try to make an effort to talk to the kids who were seated across from her.

We got through the dinner, went back to her dorm, and immediately noticed that when Sande and I had been attending parent functions, thinking Krissy was unpacking, daughter number two hadn't unpacked a single item. Not even a sock.

Sande and I looked at each other. This was going to be tougher than we thought.

I did one of the toughest things I've ever done as a father: I left her there anyway.

"Honey," I told her, "I know you're unhappy and upset with us and you want to come home, but I'm not going to take you out of here. This is a new situation, and you've never been one to love new situations. I believe in you, and my guess is this college is going to work out, but here's my guarantee: if you still feel the same way in two weeks, I will personally fly out and bring you home."

Krissy had to leave for one last brief student meeting. While she was gone, I quickly wrote her a note that she could read after I left. I told her how proud I was of her, how confident I was that she was going to be okay. Later, she told me that when she read that letter, she "cried her eyes out." She needed me to be firm, but she also needed me to be tender. The letter accomplished both.

Over the next fourteen days, we received several calls and

letters from Krissy. Two weeks to the day after we dropped her off, I phoned her.

"Well, Krissy," I said, "your two weeks are up."

There was a pause, then a confused, "What two weeks?"

"Krissy," I said, incredulous, "the two weeks. Do you want me to fly out there and bring you home?"

"Dad," Krissy answered, sounding every bit like the teenager she was, "get real." She went on to tell me how wonderful school was. Her freshman class had gone to downtown Chicago (the Loop), she was meeting new friends, enjoying her classes . . .

For once, the psychologist and his lovely bride played it right. We had based our decision on knowing Krissy's personal makeup, her individual bent. We didn't treat Krissy like we treated Holly, nor did we treat her like I would have handled Kevin II. We treated Krissy like Krissy.

Middle-borns tend to march to the beat of a different drummer. As the firstborn goes, the middle-born goes the opposite way. They're the hardest of all birth orders to pin down because children are always influenced most by what is directly above them. The middle-born looks up and sees not adults as the firstborn does, but the firstborn.

> Middle-borns tend to march to the beat of a different drummer.

How can a middle-born compete with a star performer like the firstborn? She can't. So she's smart enough to decide to take an entirely opposite direction. That's why your middle-born and firstborn daughters will differ like day and night in interests and personality.

To make things worse, when the baby of the family is born, the middle-born not only is looking at that star firstborn and knowing she can't compete but also is feeling that she can't compete with the "cuteness" of the baby of the family. No wonder middle-borns will tend to go outside their families for friendships and are less likely to confide in family members. They're relational masters, great at mediating and negotiating, since they're always stuck in the middle at home. They also tend to be more secretive, independent, diplomatic, and compromising in social situations.

Middle-borns realize that life isn't fair, because they've experienced it at home, being caught between siblings. They tend to be realistic, unspoiled risk takers who strike out on their own and know how to get along with others. They're peacemakers who are great at seeing issues from both sides.

Again, the very qualities that make them great at what they do can become negatives. Middle-borns may be suspicious or cynical because they've been ignored by their families. They may feel inferior because they're neglected. They may also rebel because they feel they don't fit in. Family members may see them as stubborn, bullheaded, or unwilling to cooperate. Since they want peace at any price, others can take advantage of them. Wanting not to offend their friends can cloud good judgment and decisions. They also may take a long time to admit they need help since it isn't easy to share feelings with family members.

Does this sound like your middle-born daughter? Since a middle-born so often gets the end of the stick—squeezed between the crown princess and little schnooky—work hard to affirm her and draw her out. If you want to give your middle-born a treat she won't forget, spend time with just her. Even better, do it on a regular basis she can count on. Don't include any other siblings, no matter how much they beg. And make sure you take plenty of pictures, since middle-borns have a lot fewer pictures in their photo albums than the firstborns and babies of the family they compete with. Take a peek at your family albums, and you'll see exactly what I mean.

Hannah

I've watched all my girls go in different directions. Let's face it: some you worry about a little more than the others. Hannah is our fourth-born child and was the baby of the family for more than five years before Lauren was born, starting, in essence, a new family.

Rewind to when Hannah was ten years old and I dropped her off at school one morning. I kissed her good-bye and watched her gather up her things into her backpack and put her backpack on. Then off she headed in the general direction of school. She was twenty steps away when her flute came flying out of her backpack and landed on the school lawn. I thought she'd hear it fall, look back, and pick it up. But she continued. Another few feet, and a book fell out. Then another book. So now three personal items of hers were on the turf.

I stretched my hand toward her and then looked skyward. I pleaded with God, *Please keep your eye on Hannah.*

Today Hannah is the most easygoing, patient, and even-tempered of our kids. She also has many of the graces her mother has. She's a marketing manager for a nonprofit that works mainly in Africa, and she does a great job with walking the line between the American and African cultures with friendly ease.

This week, as Hannah and I were talking, she said to me, "Dad, do you remember the night you woke me up at midnight for basketball?"

I couldn't help but smile. "I sure do."

The Leman family members are big sports fans—especially of the University of Arizona. Back in 1997 the Wildcats won the national basketball championship for the very first time. A huge celebration was scheduled in McKale Center, for eight or nine o'clock in the evening, as I recall. I was going to take Hannah with me to the celebration. She was so excited.

Then the news reported that the plane was going to be delayed. The players wouldn't arrive until after midnight. Hannah was ten years old at that time.

When Mama Bear heard the time got changed, she said, "Hannah, honey, you can't go. That's too late, and you have school the next day."

Hannah went to bed that night very upset and crying.

"But, Dad," she told me this week, "I remember you woke me up at midnight. You scratched my back and whispered, 'Hannah, get dressed. We're going to go to McKale Center.'" She laughed. "That was one of the most fun things we ever did."

There were fifteen thousand people at the event, with an additional overflow crowd. The sports fans were absolutely giddy and went ballistic, as only sports fans can. But Hannah told me the next day was even better than the event itself; she was a tad bit sleepy but said it was worth it. All the kids at school were talking about the reception and bemoaning the fact that they didn't get to go because it was so late. Then Hannah said, "My daddy woke me up, and we went, just the two of us." The kids dropped their jaws.

"That meant so much to me, Dad," she said. "It made me feel so special. I was the coolest kid in school that day."

Hannah is one of my four daughters. I once asked all the kids to enter their names in my new cell phone. One of the kids entered the name *Favorite daughter*. That kid was Hannah. As a dad, you want all your kids to feel like they're your favorite.

And they are—all in their own unique ways.

Everybody applauds for a firstborn star in nearly every area of life, and a middle-born has a whole group of loyal friends, but the baby of the family has her work cut out for her. She has to figure out how to get attention, so she's likely to be the most social of your kids. She's charming, people-oriented, affectionate, engaging, and tenacious—that's because she's learned early in life how to push her parents' and siblings' buttons to get what she wants. She's uncomplicated and not hard to figure out, unlike the middle-born. She tends to be the one in the family who has one or more pet names, versus the older kids, who are most likely called by their given names.

> Last-borns are likable, fun to be around, easy to talk to, caring, and lovable, and they want to help.

People love last-borns. After all, they are likable, fun to be around, easy to talk to, caring, and lovable, and they want to help. They don't have any hidden agendas, and they're often entertaining and funny. They know how to get noticed. And they don't take no for an answer; they keep going until they get what they want. Again, they spent a lot of time manipulating their older siblings to do things for them, so they've got that sort of negotiation down pat.

Last-borns are very good at working a daddy over into giving them what they want by batting eyelashes or letting a single tear slip. I've seen rock-hard negotiators, known in the business world for forcing grown men into humble compliance, melt before a teary-eyed three-year-old daughter.

Their downside? Babies of the family can come across as fly-by-the-seat-of-their-pants, or even a little flaky, impatient, spoiled, or temperamental. They're used to others pitching in and helping out with their workload (after all, those older siblings can do things more easily and faster because they already have a track record of doing them), so they can be lazy. They're also very trusting. Others can easily take advantage of them since they make decisions based on their feelings.

Does this sound like your baby-of-the-family daughter? Sure, she's charming, and she steals your heart. But if you let her manipulate you, she'll be drawn toward someone like you—somebody she can manipulate and control. So, do your future son-in-law a favor. Teach her responsibility and hold her accountable for her actions. If you do, your warm, cheerful daughter will gain the organization, compassion, and understanding she needs to make a significant impact in her adult world.

Lauren

The last child in our family, Lauren is essentially a firstborn in temperament since she spent more than five years in our home by herself. Yet, because she's the youngest in our family of five kids, she also has some entertaining, baby-of-the-family qualities.

Remember how Holly awoke in the mornings? Contrast that with Lauren, our youngest, who actually slept in her crib in our walk-in closet the summers we spent in New York. Sometimes we'd be downstairs when she woke up, and we'd hear her singing happily to herself. When we went upstairs to get her, she always had a huge smile for us.

When Lauren was in kindergarten, we got a call from school— the kind parents never want to get. "I'm sorry to inform you that we can't find your daughter."

A while later they called back to say they'd found her.

During recess, the kindergarteners had played freeze tag. It's the game where, if somebody touches you, you have to stay until somebody unfreezes you. The little girl Lauren normally played with—her partner in crime—was home sick that day. So when the whistle blew, her partner wasn't there to notice that Lauren was still standing on the corner of the playground frozen stiff. She wouldn't move. After all, the rules were that you had to be touched before you could move. That's a firstborn/only born—playing by the rules.

Today Lauren is in college. She won an $80,000 scholarship to attend. A self-starter, she launched two businesses on etsy.com: LByours and MiniatureLiterature. She makes the coolest jewelry. People old and young love it. She's profoundly creative, inventive, meticulous, and detailed. She's not a kid you have to hound or give a lot of direction to. She has great judgment, knowing right from wrong big-time. She's compassionate toward other people, an ideal young woman.

Only-born children have the positive and negative traits of firstborns times ten. They're super-achievers, perfectionists, and conscientious to the max. By the time they're eight or nine, they're pint-sized adults. They relate more to adults than to kids their own age, and they're ahead of everyone in the game of life. They don't need anyone to organize them, make plans for them, or take care of things for them.

> Only-born children have the positive and negative traits of firstborns times ten.

But those very traits that make them highly successful in their careers can also be damaging in their relationships. Their accuracy, detail, and perfectionism can work against them unless only children learn how to manage their own expectations.

Does this sound like your only-born? If so, do her three favors: Lighten up on her (especially if you tend to have that critical eye). Teach her compassion toward others and to recognize that what others think and feel is important. Find something to laugh with her about every day. If you do even those three simple things, you'll give your only-born the kind of wings that will allow her to soar for a lifetime.

Pop Quiz Time

How well do you know your school-age daughter and her world?

1. Who is your daughter's homeroom teacher?
2. What's her toughest subject?
3. What did she wear yesterday? (Be more specific than "clothing.")
4. What's her favorite musician or music group?
5. Who is her best friend? Her latest crush?
6. What does her bedroom smell like?
7. What is her absolute favorite food?
8. What is her pediatrician's or doctor's name?

Does Your Duckling Follow You?

Let's go back to Papa and Mama Duck and their ducklings from earlier in this chapter. An Austrian zoologist, Konrad Lorenz, did a fascinating study on imprinting. He divided a grouping of eggs laid by a goose. One group he left with Mama Goose; the other group was hatched in an incubator. The babies hatched by Mama followed her around, but the group hatched by the incubator followed Lorenz. Why? Researcher Eckhard H. Hess says that, "When ducklings are hatched, the first moving object they see is usually their mother. They proceed to follow her. If they see another moving object, however, they follow it instead."[1]

Just as there is a critical imprinting period in a duckling's life, the early experience of a human being is also critical. Researchers came up with three theories:

1. "Early habits are very persistent and may prevent the formation of new ones."
2. "Early perceptions deeply affect all future learning."
3. "Early social contacts determine adult social behavior."[2]

According to AnimalBehaviour.net, imprinting in ducklings occurs twenty-four to forty-eight hours after hatching. "In a variety of experiments, young chicks and ducklings were imprinted on humans, wooden blocks and classically even old gum boots. They bonded with a single item and would follow it wherever it went . . . [and would] go on to form a life-long association."[3] Even more intriguing, imprinting is irreversible.

Although the period of imprinting in human beings isn't as sharply defined as the imprinting period in birds, researchers believe it may lie somewhere within the first six months of life.[4]

Do you see, Dad, why it's so critical that you spend time with your children while they are young? Why you need to step up to the plate to help your wife with that newly out-of-the-womb baby and infant? Why you need to be available to that toddler, that elementary-age daughter, that middle schooler? If you want to make a difference in your daughter's life, you must spend time "imprinting" on her—your values, your priorities, your perspective. The longer you wait, the more difficult it becomes to imprint on your child. Your duckling will follow someone. Don't you want that someone to be you?

The time your daughter spends growing up in your home is a critical period in which the family connection needs to happen. Your daughter needs to feel love, security, and acceptance . . . from you.

> You only get one shot at fatherhood, so make it your best shot.

Take it from a father of four daughters—those little girls grow up awfully quick. If your daughter is still at the stage where she comes bounding to your arms, hugs your neck, and slathers you with kisses in welcome, enjoy those times!

You only get one shot at fatherhood, so make it your best shot. Give it all the gusto you can. Your girl deserves an involved dad.

How to Know Your Daughter

Dad, how well do you know your daughter? Have you noted her quirks? Her personality? What she's afraid of? What makes her laugh? What she's interested in?

You're a guy, and men use a lot fewer words than women. We also are masters of CliffsNotes. We want the highlights, not the blow-by-blow whole story.

Sande and I were in the car one day when Hannah phoned us. I picked up. "Hey, honey, what's new?"

"My roommate, Becca, got engaged!" she said with enthusiasm.

"Cool. She's engaged. That's nice," I responded.

Sande grabbed the phone and went off the chart with excitement. "Ohh," she squealed, "do you like the ring? Is it yellow gold, white gold, or platinum?" With nary a pause, the questions started flowing rapid-fire: "Do her parents like him? Have they set a date for the wedding? Is it going to be a big wedding? Are you in it? Has she thought about the dress yet? . . ."

She rattled off at least fifteen things I would never have thought to ask.

If I were going to ask my daughter about the wedding, what would I ask her? It would take me an hour even to compose the questions. Even then, the questions I could come up with would be very different. They'd be things like:

"Hey, she's not even old enough to be married. How old is she anyway?"

"She's twenty-two, Dad," Hannah would say with her mother's imperious tone.

That's still not old enough, I'd be thinking. And then I'd think, *Does her father have a gun?* And other assorted things such as, *I hope there aren't going to be swans at the wedding* and *I hope this isn't giving you any ideas.*

To me, this conversation was so over-the-top that I didn't even know how to relate to my wife or daughter. But contrast that to my wife, who was deliriously, genuinely thrilled that Becca was engaged.

> Dad, let me point out the obvious: your girl is not a boy.

No wonder so many men shrink and say nothing at wedding time. They know they have absolutely nothing to offer.

Dad, let me point out the obvious: your girl is not a boy. She thinks differently than you do. She talks differently than you do. She responds emotionally differently than you do.

That won't make your relationship always easy to maneuver, but it'll certainly never be boring.

Your duckling needs you to realize that not only does she need words from you, she needs sentences and full paragraphs. She also needs you to listen patiently to far more details about her life and her friends' lives than you might innately feel comfortable with. You need to step confidently into areas where many men might fear to tread. But you must do it, for the love of your duckling.

Mike, a thirty-one-year-old dad, approached me with a unique problem. "Uh, Dr. Leman," he said hesitatingly, "you told us in the seminar that we should enter our daughters' worlds. My daughter is seven, and she eats, sleeps, and breathes ballet. So how exactly am I supposed to enter her world?"

I laughed. "Well, you wouldn't look good in a pink tutu. But you can go to all her performances, watch her twirl in the living room, and even research costumes and other ballet shows with her online."

Mike shot me a note a month later to tell me he'd taken his daughter to a special performance of *Swan Lake* with a Russian theater company in a nearby city. Even better, one of his coworkers, also a dad, brought his daughter.

Now that's a dad who loves his daughter enough to risk asking another guy to go to what some less secure men would call a "poufy" event. Way to go, Mike. Your daughter will never forget what you did for her. She'll be telling the story when she's eighty to her grandkids, who'll be listening with wide eyes.

Matt is the father of two girls—Stephanie, who is almost two, and Kendra, who is four. He came from a home where his mother raised him and his brother; his father was largely absent. But Matt decided early on in his parenting that he wanted life to be different for his daughters. When he noticed recently that Stephanie loved to stack things, he took her to the store, and together they picked out a bright set of wood building blocks. That's their most fun daddy-daughter activity . . . seeing what they can build together. "My two girls are as different as day and night," Matt says. "Kendra loves to draw. I can only do stick figures." But every evening you'll find the two of them, bellies on the kitchen floor, with a long, white sheet of paper and either crayons or pencils. Matt proudly posts some of their drawings on the wall in his office.

Then there's Luther, whose daughter is a piano prodigy at age fifteen. "I can only play the radio," he says. Yet he's worked hard to arrange his work schedule so he can be at nearly all of her concerts and recitals. This past week he even took her to a huge music warehouse that was having a sale. "It was like entering a completely foreign world to me," he admits, "but my daughter absolutely loved it. I walked away with only a few bucks out of my pocket and a beaming daughter who couldn't wait to tell her mother all about our exciting outing."

Stefan is a single dad whose wife died four years ago. Their two daughters are now eleven and twelve and are interested in makeup. He hasn't a clue which end of the lipstick tube to use. So he garnered the help of Melanie, a close female friend of his wife's, who has acted like an aunt to the girls all their lives. He gave her seventy-five bucks, told her to take the girls to pick out some makeup, and then told the girls he'd have a surprise awaiting them at home when they returned. The gleeful girls returned with their makeup items to a transformed kitchen. He had moved his big dresser mirror to the table, propped it against the wall with a sign—"Makeup Party"—attached to it, and added some streamers and a roll of paper towels to clean up the mess. He had even ordered a pizza and breadsticks and cut them in small pieces for "fancy hors d'oeuvres" and served Strawberry-Banana V8 juice in their mother's fanciest crystal goblets. I can guarantee you those girls won't ever forget what their dad did for them.

And for Stefan and the girls, there was another bonus. His creativity and love for his girls so touched Melanie's heart that her steadily growing admiration for him turned into love. In three months she and Stefan will be married. The girls, who will both be bridesmaids, couldn't be more excited about Melanie joining their family because they know their mom loved her too.

So, Dad, what is your daughter interested in? How might you enter her world this week? There's nothing more manly than being the dad your daughters need you to be . . . even if you do feel like you have to go to the gym and lift weights or go on a nice, long, hot, sweaty run afterward to get your testosterone moving again.

The time to start is now. Don't wait. As my friend Anne Ortlund said, "Children are like wet cement." However, as they get older, that cement starts to harden, and change comes at a slower pace. Your daughter may be two, four, ten, fifteen, nineteen, or twenty-six. Whatever age and stage she is, you're still in the driver's seat to steer the daddy-daughter connection. It starts with individual love and forming a relationship.

Top Four Do's for Dads

1. Listen to her.
2. Take your cues from her.
3. Don't assume anything . . . ever.
4. Be gentle.

The Power of Individual Love

When you get to know your daughter as an individual, it will become second nature for you to act in a way that works best with her birth-order traits and her personality. For an example, I'll take you back to our second daughter, Krissy, and her transition-to-college experience.

Because I knew Krissy well, I realized it wouldn't be fair to abandon her at North Park, even though she had begun to settle in after those first couple of rough weeks. I knew it would only be a matter of time before she started feeling homesick. So, since I travel a lot for business, I decided to make it a regular practice to arrange for long layovers in Chicago. The airlines will allow you to stay at an airport for up to four hours before you catch the next plane without charging you for that airport being a separate destination.

The first time I did this, I wanted it to be special, so I arrived at the school without giving Krissy advance notice. (Now, if that would have been Holly, our firstborn, I would have had to inform her down to the minute when I'd be arriving. See what I mean about treating your daughters differently?) I had to go to Old Main to find out where Krissy would be, and I made sure to give myself enough time to get there before she did. I learned she was scheduled to be in a cell biology class, which met in an auditorium.

Ten minutes later, she was walking toward class when she saw her old man hanging out front. Her jaw dropped open, her face lit up, and the love that illuminated her face made me so glad I had taken the time to show up.

"How'd you know where I'd be?" she cried out.

"I went to Old Main and asked them."

"That is so cool," she said, incredulous.

She felt special. For those two and a half hours, she knew she was in the center of her father's heart. We had a great time eating lunch, talking, and catching up on each other's lives. Sure, we'd had letters and phone calls in between, but there's nothing like being able to look each other directly in the eyes.

> For those two and a half hours, she knew she was in the center of her father's heart.

This continued throughout Krissy's stay in college. During Krissy's sophomore year, Sande and I went to Mexico. I spoke to the Young Presidents' Organizations at their YPO University. We knew from Krissy's letters that she was facing another down time, so on the return trip home I convinced the airline to give us a ticket that would take us from Mexico City to Arizona via the convenient route of Chicago! You have to have a bevy of frequent flyer miles to get that favor, but once it was done, we eagerly anticipated the surprise.

Knowing how young women hate to be embarrassed, especially by their parents, Sande and I showed up at Krissy's dorm wearing sombreros and Mexican blankets. Of course, as a baby of the family myself, it was my idea; Sande, my classy firstborn wife, agreed to play along not only because she loves me but because she's been worn down to my crazy ideas over the years.

We fit into the Chicago, academic yuppie scene about as well as a ham dinner at a synagogue. Wanting to really spring the surprise, we simply passed on the following message: *Tell Krissy Leman she has a package waiting for her downstairs.*

When Krissy came down to get her package, there were the two amigos!

You may have one daughter; you may have five daughters. But the important thing is to study each daughter's character and apply a distinct style of parenting that fits her personality.

Don't fall for "even-steven parenting," which treats all kids alike, no matter their specific needs. Instead, try to make each child feel special. Those methods have paid big dividends in our relationships with our daughters.

Sande and I received tremendous affirmation on the day Krissy was married. Krissy told her big sis, Holly—her maid of honor—in a letter that she was a little nervous about getting married first. She also acknowledged Holly's role as the firstborn with affection, rather than competition. Here's some of what she said to her sister:

> Study each daughter's character and apply a distinct style of parenting that fits her personality.

> You've always gone first. And I never have liked going first. That's probably why God gave me such a special sister like you. It can't be easy being at the top, knowing your four siblings are all looking up to you. I want you to know how very special you are to me and how I treasure all the memories. I love you with all of my heart. Thank you for standing next to me as I marry Den. It means so much to me that you're there. Thanks for being so special. I pray we will always remain close in heart, even though we'll be living in different states. I love you! Kris.

As a father, holding this letter in my hand was one of those rare moments where I realized that Krissy's wet cement had hardened, and the result is that two once-warring siblings have grown to love and appreciate each other in adulthood. Their relationship will stand the test of time, even when Sande and I are long gone.

Few things in life have been as rewarding as getting to know each of my daughters' quirks, fears, dreams, and hopes, and then parenting around those. When you do that, Dad, you make your daughter feel special. Like the notorious bandit El Guapo tells his men in what I consider the greatest of all movies, *The Three Amigos,* "I know each of you like I know my own smell."

Sande says I have a nose like a beagle. That has come in handy in dealing with my daughters and distinguishing between them. But like every other dad, when my second child was born, I had at first assumed that she would be a clone of the first one. Was I ever wrong! My two girls were night-and-day different from day one.

When you know your daughter like you know your own smell, loving her as an individual will be a natural response, as simple as breathing. You'll also make decisions that are right for her, and you'll be on your way to building a relationship for a lifetime.

A Good Dad's Quick Reference Guide

- Know and love your daughter as an individual.
- Make her feel special.

FOUR

Walking the Balance Beam

There's nothing more important in life than living a disciplined, balanced lifestyle—for you or your daughter.

Who doesn't love to watch the Olympics? They're so inspiring. Some of my daughters' favorite events have been the gymnastic ones. We sweat with the performers over their floor routines and wince at a misstep or a bounce that goes out of bounds. But we all collectively hold our breath when the athletes are on the balance beam, where one tiny wobble could end an Olympic career, or a dismount could go awry at the last second.

Dad, every day you are walking the balance beam with your daughter. On that narrow beam of life, everything is about balance. There's nothing more important than living a disciplined lifestyle, since it affects everything about your present and your future. But here's the catch: if you want your daughter to live a disciplined lifestyle, you have to live that way yourself.

When Andrew's daughter, Kristal, asked him if she could go to the school dance with a guy friend from school, he came unglued. "You are only fourteen years old, and you are not going to any dance with any boy for a very long time. I can't even believe you'd bring that up." He continued to rip into her until she burst into tears and ran off to her room, slamming the door.

Ouch. That kind of "I'll huff and I'll puff and I'll blow the door down" parental behavior will do nothing for your relationship with your daughter. Sure, your dad might have done it to you, but I've got news for you. It's not going to help your relationship with your daughter, especially at this stage in a game where she's trying to tell you nicely she's interested not only in the dance but in that boy who has caught her eye too.

Thankfully, Andrew didn't leave the situation there. After several more minutes of huffing and puffing, Andrew caught himself. He realized that he'd done exactly what he used to do, and what his father had done to him—without thinking. It had come naturally. But the result was that he had effectively shut his daughter down.

Do you think she'll ask her dad about a dance again? Or will she be more likely to sneak out the door and go, to avoid all the hoopla of the huffing, puffing, big, bad wolf? If you make it a pattern to shut your daughter down, eventually she'll find a way to get back at you, which includes doing exactly the opposite of what you've told her to do. It's called human nature, and you're not the only one who has it.

So after Andrew winced and realized what he did, and thought through what he should have done—open ears and disengage mouth, for starters—he knew he had to go to talk with his daughter. First, he needed to apologize.

If you were that dad who blew his top, what would you say?

Take a minute to think it through before you continue reading . . .

Here's what happened next in Andrew's story. He walked to his daughter's room, heard her crying, and knocked softly on the door. "Uh, Kristal, can I talk to you?"

"I don't want to talk to you!" she shouted back. "Go talk to Mom!"

Andrew did and found out, to his misery, that Kristal had already run the dance idea by her mom, and her mom had already blessed it. In fact, it was the son of a family friend who had invited her to the school dance. Ouch. Now he had two unhappy women in the house.

Andrew realized he'd overreacted based on his view of "Daddy's little girl." He'd like to keep her six forever, but checking the calendar, he noted she really was fourteen. In fact, she'd be fifteen in less than a month, and ready for driver's ed. Where had the time gone?

A very humble Andrew knocked on his daughter's door this time to say he was sorry. Then he said, "Wow, a dance. Sounds interesting. Tell me more about it."

As soon as a dad says that, he goes into the smart dad column, and that's the column you want to be in. Because if you're in the dumb-daddy column, she's not going to listen to you. She'll give you lip service and maybe flip you a bone of information, but that's all.

Think back for a second. What were you doing when you were in middle school? I'm old, so I have to think way back. When I was twelve and in the seventh grade, I went to a Halloween dance and danced ever so closely with a girl during the "Broomstick Bounce." We shared apple cider and doughnuts too. Later that girl, Wendy, would become my best buddy Moonhead's wife.

> Think back for a second. What were you doing when you were in middle school?

We parents are very good at overreacting to situations . . . or letting situations go rather than addressing them because they might feel too messy. But there is a much better way.

What Kind of Parent Are You?

There are three basic kinds of parents. See if you can identify your own parents and yourself in one or more of the following scenarios.

The Authoritarian Parent

"I'm the parent. I'm in charge here."

"Eat it. It's good for you."

"Get your backpack—now. Under no circumstances will you be late for school again."

Many of us grew up with the authoritarian view of parenting, which says that adults are bigger—and therefore better—than kids. The authoritarian parent is the one who holds rigid control over his family. He doesn't give his daughter any room to have her own opinion; what he wants goes. The only thing that matters is what he thinks. He holds the hammer of parental authority above his daughter's head. But by acting like his way is the only way and attempting to be powerful, he only comes across as close-minded. That behavior shuts his daughter off . . . and effectively shuts down their relationship. Trying to dominate kids might work when they're young and you're physically more powerful than they are. However, power and control beget power and control. Somewhere along the line, the daughter of an authoritarian parent will make him pay in more ways than he can imagine.

Juvenile detention cells are full of teenage girls who say, "My dad never listened. He never cared. He wanted everything his way and only his way."

Too many teenage girls are experiencing pregnancy out of wedlock because they're searching for the daddy connection—the warmth and the love—that their own father didn't provide for them in his own quest for power and control.

Many of the results of this parenting style are tragic indeed. The time for a change is now.

The Permissive Parent

"Whatever I can do to serve you."

"Oh, you want to go right now? Well, of course. I'll drop everything I'm doing and take you."

"You want the car keys? Okay. By the way, I'll take care of those two speeding tickets for you tomorrow on my lunch break."

"My daughter isn't rebellious, she's just . . ."

The permissive parents are the "anything goes" type and the "fixers." Some parents are very good at turning their daughters into power brokers by trying to make sure they're happy at every turn. But all that does is create a kid who thinks she's at the center of the universe—a kid whose whims hold everyone around her hostage.

Take, for instance, Mary, a nine-year-old girl who worked hard to be top dog of her school class. Problem was, her way of doing that was by threatening and intimidating other girls in the class. Because her parents always covered for her and rationalized her behavior, Mary never learned that actions have consequences. When Mary was twelve, she backed a girl around the corner at school and threatened her with a knife. Thankfully, a teacher came around the corner, and Mary tucked the knife back in her pocket while the other girl fled. But the other girl's parents reported Mary and brought an attorney with them to

school. This time Mary's parents couldn't change the consequences. Mary was suspended from school and is now in juvenile
hall, awaiting next steps since many other girls and their families
are now coming forward to act as witnesses to Mary's bullying.
This example may seem extreme, but it's real life. However, it's a
direct result of permissive parents trying to smooth Mary's road
in life at junctures all along the way, when what that little girl
needed was some tough love and major attitude and behavior
adjustments. Now the entire family has a wake-up call.

New York Times writer Lisa Belkin noted that cheating, lying,
and stealing are on the rise, and asks, "Does the problem start at
home? With parents who wear blinders and, directly or obliquely,
encourage moral ambiguity?"[1] As a result of that article, a reader,
Wendy, actually invited the police into her home after her
seventeen-year-old daughter had stolen her ATM card multiple
times and made purchases without permission. A police officer
came over, handcuffed her daughter, and had her sit in the back
of the police car while explaining what a felony was and what
happens to people who steal.

Why did Wendy do it? Here's what she said:

> Everyone makes mistakes. I'd rather my daughter learn the
> consequences of serious errors while those consequences are
> still small and not life-altering. It's sad to watch a kid with
> such potential suffer but it felt good to know I didn't excuse
> her behavior, accept it, tolerate it, or make excuses. Burying
> my head in the sand does my children a huge disservice. If they
> don't learn to make good choices while in my home, society
> will teach them to obey the law. I know I can say I love her
> enough to help her stay on the straight and narrow path—the
> one that leads to freedom and happiness.[2]

Contrast Mary's parents' behavior and Wendy's behavior. Do you really want to be ruled by your kid? The sooner your daughter learns that life isn't all about her, and that other people's ideas and opinions matter, the better for you, for her, and for the rest of the world.

Often when there's an authoritarian parent in the home, there's also a permissive parent in the home. Usually the authoritarian tends to be Dad, while the permissive parent tends to be Mom, who wants to make her kids happy but in fact enables them.

Either extreme of parenting isn't beneficial to a daughter's well-being. And it's even worse when the permissive parent allows the daughter to control the situation behind the authoritarian's back.

The Authoritative Parent

The authoritative parent is a balanced parent who understands that each child is different. Some children will knuckle under and be repentant with a single glance of parental displeasure. Others will get defiantly in your face to secure what they want. The authoritative parent knows how to navigate both personalities to bring the best out of each daughter.

Your daughter may not always like you, but she needs the guidelines you provide for her because they mean safety. Without those boundaries, she will feel insecure about her role in the family and her place in the world.

The authoritative parent realizes that God Almighty hasn't made one person better than the other, but we as parents have lived longer than our kids and thus know more about the consequences for our actions. We also have a differing role of responsibilities.

Dad, you're the adult here, so act like it. Because you love your daughter, you provide her with the basic amenities of life—food, shelter, and an iPhone. But what she needs most is your steady, guiding hand and your unconditional love. She needs you to straightforwardly and kindly tell it like it is when she needs a wake-up call. And she also needs you to know that, when she's somewhere she doesn't want to be, the first person she can call, with no questions asked, is her daddy, who will come get her.

That's a relationship you can stake a lifetime on.

But how does it play out in real life?

Let's go back to Andrew, the dad whose daughter, Kristal, wanted to go to the dance. What he really needs to do now is come alongside his daughter when she buys that special dress for the dance and say, "Wow, that dress is a home run. It looks great on you. You made a fabulous choice." A dad who gives his daughter the male admiration she longs for will be giving her a gift for a lifetime. If you don't treat your daughter with respect and admiration, then some guy who doesn't have her best in mind is going to say admiring things to her—things you don't want to hear about. Without your affirmation, the chances of your daughter falling into that snare are much higher.

Parents create problems if they edge toward either side of the spectrum—the authoritarian/dictator, or the permissive/ anything-goes parent. If you're married, you need to be on the same page with your spouse regarding discipline. Mom and Dad need to discuss things before actions are taken, because if you say something is going to happen, it must happen. If you lay down the law, you must be willing to abide by it. Otherwise, your inconsistency undermines your daughter's security. If rules are always changing or your daughter can manipulate you, her world becomes unstable and fearful. Taking time to think through the consequences first—both what they mean to you and to your daughter—will help you make wise decisions when you're in the heat of battle. Your kids need to know not only what the parameters are but also what will happen if those parameters are not met.

If you're a tough guy and your wife is permissive, then you're fighting a forest fire with a garden hose. Your kids will be miserable, yanked back and forth between two opposite sides of parenting. You lay down the law, and then your wife quietly negates that law behind your back, because she feels bad for the kids. Or you grant permission for your daughter to do something, and then your wife yanks it back from her, denying your daughter the chance to do something you'd already approved and that she already believed was hers to do. When your kids find themselves in this situation, they will then learn how to effectively play you off of each other, which won't have good results in your marriage.

> Parents create problems if they edge toward either side of the spectrum—the authoritarian/ dictator, or the permissive/ anything-goes parent.

Here's what I mean. You've issued a fatherly edict that your twelve-year-old daughter is grounded until the weekend for sassing her mother for the umpteenth time in one day. How would you feel if you headed out the door for your son's baseball practice, and you overheard the following conversation between your wife and your daughter?

WIFE: Hang in there. Wait until Dad's out the door and then I'll take you to the mall with your friends like you'd planned. But we have to be back in less than two hours, before Dad and Sean are back.

DAUGHTER: Okay, but you'd better drive fast. I can't be late.

Wouldn't you feel more than a little betrayed by your wife, who is undercutting your authority? Even worse, she deserves all your daughter dishes out since she can't stand up for herself. After all, you did what you did—grounded your daughter—to try to gain some respect from your daughter toward your wife. But if your permissive wife allows herself to be treated with disrespect, and even encourages it via her actions, nothing will change. The daughter is continuing to manipulate the situation. And now she's got Mom even more over a barrel, since Mom is doing something that Dad forbade. As Sir Walter Scott said, "Oh! what a tangled web we weave / When first we practise to deceive!"[3] Sadly, the above scenario plays out in many homes across the country. If it's playing out in yours, you need to read my book *Parenting the Powerful Child.* It scratches where parents itch today.

When my wife and I talked about parenting, we agreed that we had to have a united front with our kids. We came up with a list of certain standards of behavior that we expected our kids to adhere to, and we trained our kids to those standards. I knew that I could take my kids to any person's house and they would never walk into the living room and stand on their couch. How do I know that? Because I know my kids. I trained them to be respectful of other people's property. There are specific things they would do and not do. They'd never jump on our furniture, so they certainly wouldn't jump on someone else's furniture.

I have a banner on my website BirthOrderGuy.com that reads: PARENTING ISN'T EASY, BUT IT'S SIMPLE. You've got to have a simple game plan, with both parents on the same page and acting in an authoritative manner. Add in unconditional love, acceptance, and cooperation, and you've got a wonderful, nurturing, noncompetitive environment for your daughter to grow up in.

What kind of daughter do you want? Make a list. In fact, stop right now and do it.

Do you want her to be responsible? Then give her responsibility. Be responsible yourself.

Do you want her to be kind? Then show her kindness and insist that she be kind to her siblings. Even more, show kindness yourself to others. For example, if a driver is trying to get in line on a busy freeway feeder, what do you do? Speed up and try to cut the guy off, or let the guy in?

Your daughter is watching. She's absorbing the words you say, your expressions, your attitude. All those things are being entered like data in the computer of your daughter's head.

How to Fight Right

- Shut your mouth.
- Listen, listen, listen.
- Don't expect instant obedience.
- Keep your voice steady. Raising it won't get you anywhere.
- Watch your own attitude. It affects hers.
- Always remember: Who died and left you boss? Her opinion is as valid as yours.

Discipline That Works

You'll never win when you choose to do battle with your child of any age. You have much more to lose than your daughter. When your kindergarten daughter pitches a fit in Walmart, does she really care what others think? No, but you do. Does your teenage daughter care if her shirt is too tight or her skirt too short? No, because that's the style and what "everybody" is wearing. But you care, and she knows it. As she parades past you and out the door, she gives you that "I dare you to do anything" look. What do you do in response?

There's a great way to establish healthy authority in your home with a child of any age. It starts with three principles.

Principle #1: Say It Once, Turn Your Back, Walk Away

When you say something one time, you're expecting the best out of your daughter and your relationship. She has ears, and she can hear you. Telling her something more than once is basically saying to her, "You're so stupid, you won't get it unless I repeat myself" or "I'm so uncomfortable calling the shots in my own home that I feel like I need to say it more than once to be heard." Neither way will help you establish that healthy authority in your home as the authoritative parent you need to be. But saying something once says, "I respect you, my daughter, and I know you hear me." When you turn your back and walk away, you're not engaging in a battle of any kind.

After all, it takes two to tango, and you don't need to do that dance, nor should you, with your daughter. How does this principle work?

For example, when that young daughter pitches a fit in Walmart, here's what you do. Exhale heavily, with your hands dramatically placed on your hips, and say to the frowning people around you, "Well! Some people's children!" Then you turn your back and walk away. I guarantee that youngster will stop her fit when she's surrounded by unfriendly eyes and Papa Bear is already moving down the aisle away from her. Before you turn the corner of the aisle, she'll be scrambling after you. After all, the fit is there for your benefit. Without your audience, it doesn't work.

Then comes the test: When she, with her repentant baby blues, says at the checkout counter, "Daddy, I want a candy bar," what do you say?

You say it once: "No, because Dad is still unhappy about what happened earlier."

Then you turn your back and start putting your other purchases on the checkout counter.

You walk out of that store without a treat, even when the "But Dad . . ." begging or whining or crying starts. At that point, you become "daughter deaf," even if the people around you are shooting daggers in your direction.

Your daughter will get two messages loudly and clearly: *Throwing fits doesn't work,* and *You don't mess with Dad. He means what he says.*

Ask Dr. Leman

Q: I have two daughters, fourteen and twelve. To say our house is a war zone, especially because we live in a small home and our daughters have to share a bedroom, is an understatement. They're always in each other's faces, and then my wife gets really stressed out. Whenever we talk about the problem, my wife begs me to stay out of it and says it'll only make things worse. But I don't want to live this way for the next four to six years until our girls go off to college or their jobs. Some help, please?

—Antony, New York

A: Good for you, because nobody should live like that. Your wife sounds like a firstborn or middle-born and a pleaser— someone who wants life's highways to be smooth. So here's what I suggest: quietly send your wife away for the weekend to her parents' or her sister's without either of you telling your girls. Tell her that you are going to problem solve between the two girls and that, since she finds the interaction stressful, you are granting her the gift of a little vacation to see what you can accomplish. Ask her not to call, text, or e-mail the girls from the minute she leaves to the minute she comes back. The last thing you need is for your girls to try to divide Mom and Dad on the issue. You don't need to end up "the bad guy" to your wife.

Arrange to be home when the girls get back from school on Friday afternoon. Have plenty of snacks and bottled water already stashed in the family room since nothing works well with preteens and teenagers if they're hungry. As soon as your daughters' backpacks hit the kitchen floor and the bickering starts, call your daughters into the family room for a meeting.

Start with words similar to this:

"Girls, I love both of you, but I don't like what is happening between you, the way you're treating each other, or how your constant fighting and bickering is turning our home into a war zone. So, tonight, neither of you are going anywhere. You are going to stay in this room until the two of you come to a mutually agreeable solution for how you are going to get along. I sent Mom away for the weekend. She will not be contacting you this weekend, nor responding to any messages from you, while we work this out. Your cell phones and iPods will stay in your backpacks in the kitchen, where you left them, for the entire weekend. We will spend Saturday and Sunday at home, together, the three of us, with no one else involved. If you cannot work this out, I'll work it out for you, and I guarantee that neither of you will like my solution."

The arguments will start: "But Dad, she . . ."

You've said your piece, so you turn your back, exit, and close the family room door if there is one. (If not, you might want to pick a different room, but not their bedroom, which is the hottest warfare territory.)

For a while you'll probably hear yelling, but then something amazing will happen. A profound silence will likely descend upon your home. If you can peek through a window in the family room without them seeing you, you'll probably see two very embarrassed girls staring at each other. You've called their bluff, and they know it.

If they try to come out early and say they're done, but they're still not looking each other in the eye and the bickering starts up again once they think you're out of range, march them right back to the family room. Sure, it'll be a long night for all of you, but do you really want this fighting to end? If so, you've got to stay tough. You've set the parameters that *they* will work this out, so you've got to stay disengaged in the fight. If they pull you back in, you're back to square one.

There's one more thing you can do. It's really important for teenagers to have their own space. Do *anything* to get those girls their own rooms, even if it's installing a makeshift wall right down the middle of their current bedroom and putting one bed on either side of it. If you have an office in the house, and you could move your desk to the family room or the basement, do so. Or if you have an unfinished basement, and could build one of the girls a bedroom there or take a corner for your office downstairs, do so. Constantly being together has no doubt helped to fuel your daughters' war. Everybody needs peace, quiet, a break from other humans, and some space to call their own. One of our daughters actually slept in a walk-in closet for a long time, but it was *her space.*

Good luck!

Antony's report, a month later

Wow, the plan really worked! That night was majorly stressful, but life has been blissful since then. My wife came home Sunday night and whispered, "Hey, what happened? It's quiet in here." She was even more shocked when she saw both girls on the couch, laughing as they watched a movie together. It took until 2:00 a.m. on Saturday for the girls to work out their solution, but they did it. The next morning they asked if they could get dividing screens for their bedroom (one of them is a mess-maker; one of them is a clean freak), and if they could clean out the hallway closet so they'd have more room for their stuff. I surprised them by telling them I'd decided to give up my office so one of them could have it as a bedroom. I said we could toss a coin as to who would get it.

"That's okay," Melissa, my younger daughter, said. "She can have it." She pointed to her older sister.

"No, it's okay," Mandy said. "It's got more windows than ours, and I know having lots of light is important to Missy since she likes to paint."

Wow, one daughter thinking of another first. I could hardly believe it. The girls helped me move my desk and used their screen idea to create an office for me in a corner of the living room. They even set up rules about when they could have the TV on so they didn't disturb my work time. I was stunned. I didn't ask them to do that. On top of that, they cleaned out the hallway closet of all their old junk and turned it into "office space" for me. They even moved my filing cabinet in there and organized all of my desk junk on the shelves for easy access.

If anyone would have told me a month ago that the change in our house could be this amazing, I'd never have believed it. But now, thanks to your suggestions, I not only believe it, I'm living it!

Here's another example. Let's say your middle schooler disses you or her mother before she dashes out the door for the school bus in the morning. Yelling after her, "Young lady, how dare you . . ." will only boost your blood pressure and start your day off with the kind of negative emotion you don't need and psychologists warn you about. As for your daughter? She'll be already on the bus, scot-free, thinking, *Hey, by the time I get home, he'll be cooled off. No biggie.*

So, Dad, you wait for that teachable moment, when your daughter wants you to drive her to her friend's house after school. You say, "Not tonight."

She looks confused. "But why? I don't have any homework tonight, and I already told Janine I could come."

Now here's the teachable moment. "I don't appreciate the way that you talked to me and your mother this morning." Then you turn your back and walk away.

Talk about heaping hot coals on your daughter. She'll apologize—if not at that moment, within a short while, because now she's got something at stake. Then she'll expect you to take her. But hold your ground, Dad. "I forgive you, and I will expect you to respond differently tomorrow morning. But no, you're still not going to Janine's tonight. It's up to you how you explain that to her." You turn your back and walk away.

That's putting the ball of responsibility in your daughter's court. She has to be the one to explain to Janine why she can't come. You've made your point, and your daughter will think through her words and actions more carefully next time because there are consequences and she knows you'll hold firm to them.

> If you want your daughter to take you seriously, say it once and only once.

So if you want your daughter to take you seriously, say it once and only once. Then turn your back, expecting your words to be followed. There's no argument, no backtalk. Everything is stated in a calm manner.

Then you walk away and get busy doing something else.

Your daughter may be mad, shocked, confused, or all of those. Believe me, she'll test you to see if this is only a fluke, because you recently read a book by some "family expert" called Dr. Kevin Leman and are trying it out. But when she sees you mean business, she'll know that there will be consequences for her action—or inaction. Even more, you, Dad, will not be talked out of those consequences. After all, if you miss a deadline at work, you have consequences, including an unhappy boss or customer. So why not teach your daughter a bit about real life while she's still in the safe environment of your home?

Principle #2: Share Your Disapproval and Your Opinion Gently

What about your sixteen-year-old daughter with the tight shirt and short skirt who makes you want to follow her to school and stand guard over her with a shotgun? You have a kind but straightforward conversation with your teenage daughter that goes something like this:

"Jessica, I know you like to wear that skirt and shirt. It's the kind of thing all your friends wear. But when you do, the boys in high school put you in a category I don't honestly believe you want to be in. I know, because I was a boy in high school once, and that's what my friends and I thought. You are worth far more than that in my eyes, and I don't want you to cheapen yourself. When I met your mother, she was all the more mysterious and intriguing to me because of what she didn't show on the surface. You're now at a place in life where many of your choices will be your own. I won't always be walking beside you, telling you what to do. You're growing up. But I want you to think very carefully about this decision, because of what it says about you and how it can influence your future, including the type of men you attract."

You say your piece, turn your back, and walk away. You do not participate in any further words at that point, because if she's a powerful personality, she'll want to fight. But when you walk away, without raising your voice, and state what you did straightforwardly, I guarantee your daughter will think about your words, even if she does wear that skirt and shirt out the door. She'll probably spend a lot of time in her room that night, going through her closet and evaluating her choices. Believe me, she heard you. At her heart, no girl wants to be a "cheap girl" in the eyes of a boy, and most particularly not in the eyes of her number-one man—you. The exception, of course, is the girl who doesn't have a positive dad or any dad in her life. Then, due to the tremendous father hunger in her, she might act and dress in a provocative way that draws guys' attention to her. The sad truth is, she'll end up with the kind of guys who reinforce her thinking that she isn't worth much, and the cycle of dysfunction continues.

The person your daughter wants to please most in the world is you, Dad. That's why even a hint of your disapproval, stated in a balanced manner, can go a long way toward turning unwanted behavior around.

Principle #3: B Doesn't Happen Before A is Completed

Let's say that you asked your daughter three days ago to do a certain task at home before the weekend so that you can accomplish what you need to do on the weekend. You come home on the fourth day, and it's still not done.

If you are an authoritarian dad, you'd whip into her bedroom and confront her. "Young lady, I *asked* you to do that three days ago, and it's still not done! What is your problem? You could at least contribute something around here. Do you think we're your slaves? I'm giving you *one hour* to get it done, and if it's not . . ." And you stalk out the door. What did you accomplish? Nothing.

If you are a permissive dad, you'd quietly do the job yourself and not say anything. After all, your daughter must have been busy. She does have a lot to do as a student . . . (even though you know for a fact she spent two hours on Facebook last night). What did you accomplish? Nothing.

If you are an authoritative dad, you wait for a teachable moment. It's Thursday night, the task still isn't done, and you know she has plans with her girlfriends on Friday night. You don't remind her; you simply wait. Friday evening, after dinner, she holds her hand out for the car keys.

"Dad, I need the keys," she says. "So I can pick up my friends for the movie."

When you pause, she prompts, "Remember?"

"Sure, I remember," you reply calmly. "I also remember that four days ago, I asked you to do [whatever it was] before the weekend, so I can start on my project tomorrow. It still isn't done."

She'll try the "Oh, I forgot. I'll do it when I get home" dog and pony show.

> She'll try the "Oh, I forgot. I'll do it when I get home" dog and pony show.

You're smart enough not to fall for it. "I asked you to do it before the weekend started. So I guess you and your friends may be a little late for that movie," you say. You then turn your back and walk away.

She panics. "But, Dad, I can't be late! They're waiting for me."

"That's okay," you say with a little humor. "I've been waiting for you to do what you need to do for four days."

Dad, you don't back down. B doesn't happen before A is completed. She won't forget next time.

But let's say in that scenario that your daughter has already left for the movie before you arrive home. Then you work in the teachable moment the following morning, using principles 2 and 3.

It might sound something like this: "Bethany, four days ago I asked you to take care of [whatever the task is] before the weekend," you say in a calm, even tone. "However, when I came home last night, you were gone to the movies with your girlfriends and it still wasn't done. So I had to do it myself. I can't tell you how disappointed I am that you didn't follow through on what I asked you to do. I don't ask you to do that many things, but when I do, those are things I need you to do without being reminded."

How does that daughter feel? Bad. She knows in her heart she was supposed to do that work. Most daughters would say, "Oh, Dad, I would have done it."

Your response? You look her straight in the eye and say, "If that were true, the task would have been done. So this morning, after breakfast, I'd like you to reflect for a while about what you'll do differently next time."

When you do that, you're disciplining your daughter in a gentle manner. You're gently raking coals over your daughter's head and making her feel a little guilty.

Let me take that back. You haven't *made* her feel guilty, but the actions you've chosen to take—good, authoritative actions— have created guilt in your daughter.

Here's the good news. It's good guilt. Now is a prime time for your daughter to get in touch with her feelings. Simply being steady and calm while showing your disapproval will sting. The next time you ask your daughter to do something, the memory of your previous action will provoke her to get that task done. And in the meanwhile, your carefully measured action will maintain a normal temperature in your home in the presence of a volatile, emotional teenage girl.

Sometimes tough love is needed. In those cases where things need to change, first evaluate yourself. What part, if anything, have you played in your daughter's responses and actions? If you have had a part, then pony up about what you did first, and apologize for it. Nothing can make you look like a bigger man in your daughter's eyes.

Then, after reflection, decide on a plan of action. If you're married, it's critical that you discuss the plan with your wife before you act. We men are very used to doing things on our own, but marriage is a partnership.

If action does need to be taken in discipline, remember that B doesn't happen until A is completed. Nothing is sacred. Not Grandma's house, not school, not the concert, an already planned outing with friends, or horse riding this weekend. Sometimes your daughter will need the rug pulled out from under her so she knows that you mean business. But remember that it is possible to be firm, and to be a man, without being harsh.

Walking that Balanced Line

In general, we as a society rear kids to make no decisions whatsoever. We snowplow their roads of life until they're smooth, make excuses for them at every turn, and do homework for them to lighten their load. We let them off the hook, not holding them accountable if they say they're going to do things and then don't follow through. We raise them to be the center of the universe, turning our kids into power brokers by trying to make them happy all the time. In many homes kids call the shots. But the catch is that we've created those children to be that way, and now we're being held hostage by them.

What we should be teaching them is responsibility and accountability and that others matter. But we can only teach what we do ourselves. Who we are shouts louder than what we say.

So dads, be careful what you say to your daughters and how you say it. Watch how you live and interact with others. If you teach your daughter the old-fashioned values of responsibility, compassion for others, and respect for herself, and you model them yourself, you set your daughter up for not only a disciplined lifestyle but healthy, balanced relationships in all areas of her life, especially with men.

Your involvement, your interest, your wisdom make all the difference to your daughter now and in the future.

A Good Dad's Quick Reference Guide

- Keep your cool.
- Balance always wins the game.

FIVE

The Birds, the Bees,
and "the Talk"

*Talking turkey to your developing daughter about
sex, the male perspective, and responsibility.*

There isn't a dad in the world who woke up this morning and
said to himself, "You know, I can't wait to have a straight
talk today with my daughter about sex and relationships."

No, the very thought of it is the way you feel when you know
you're going to the dentist for a root canal. You may not want to
do it, but it's something you know you have to do, so you steel
yourself for the painful event.

I'm going to say something now that will surprise you. Dad,
there is no one better to talk to your daughter about the birds and
the bees than you. *Wait a sec,* you're thinking, as the panic rises.
*You're throwing me a curveball here. I thought my wife would
do that. I know nothing about tampons.* Granted, your wife or
a close female friend can be in charge of the tampon brigade
and its many choices, but who better than you to talk to your

daughter about how young men see women? You know what boys are thinking and can most effectively address that. After all, you own the same equipment as those boys.

Go back in your memory bank a little. What did you think about as a young man of age nine, ten, eleven, thirteen, fifteen, seventeen, nineteen, and so on? How did you view young women? And how do you want a young man to view your daughter? Aren't there some things you could share, from a male perspective, with your daughter that would be really useful for her?

Sure, you can read a book. In fact, I've got a great one for you that will give you some additional help, more than I can give in a single chapter of this book—*A Chicken's Guide to Talking Turkey to Your Kids About Sex*, by yours truly. But nothing can replace your firsthand wisdom because of the relationship you're forming with your daughter.

"The Talk" Isn't a One-Time Event

I know a guy who doesn't fear anything. He's an ex-Army Ranger, the best fighting machine there is. A trained killer. Put him in hand-to-hand combat and he'd come out on top. But when it comes to talking to his daughter about her changing body, that tough guy sweats.

Let's admit it. We guys aren't comfortable with the flow of words the way women are. We won't talk to our girls the same way women would. Add the wrinkle of this uncomfortable topic of sex (Did you wince when you read that word? If so, this chapter is perfect for you), and we feel tongue-tied and bumbling. Many dads can only manage something like, "Uh, honey, there are some things you ought to know. I bought you a book," and they give it to their daughters. That is, if they haven't talked their wives or next-door neighbors into giving the book first.

When my daughters were young, the thought of talking with them about sex scared me. But what scared me more was this thought: *If you don't talk to your daughter about sex, you know who will?* Well, for starters, hormone-raging boys who have their own agendas. Or authors of Internet blogs who report on "Ten Ways to Have the Hottest Sex with Your Boyfriend." Or sex-ed teachers who may present greatly differing values from yours. It wouldn't be normal for your daughter to not be curious about sex. If she senses you're not open to talking about the subject, she'll go elsewhere, and you'll have absolutely no control over what she learns. The last thing your daughter needs is a lifetime of feeling "used" and "dirty" because she didn't know the truth about premarital sex beforehand. She deserves to hear about sex, as it was intended to be, from a man she trusts—you.

We were all created as sexual beings. Trying to hide that is like trying to shove an elephant underneath the carpet in your living room and ignoring the bump as you walk over it. Your job is not to run from your daughter's questions about sex, her developing figure, and the opposite gender, but to channel those queries in the right direction. Most of us fall into the trap of thinking that "the Talk"—the explanation of the birds and the bees and how all of it works—is a one-time, uncomfortable event. Instead it's an ongoing process that should start at a young age and develop age-appropriately with your daughter.

How I Did It

When my daughters were younger, the last words they wanted to hear out of my mouth were *sex, penis,* or *vagina.* They even said out loud, "Dad, I really don't want to be hearing this."

But they heard it anyway. We didn't have a one-time sex talk. We had regular talks that came up in the normal course of life, so they had plenty of opportunities to pretend they didn't want to discuss the more private aspects of being a sexual being.

However, I knew the truth. They were curious. Even though they rolled their eyes, inside, they were saying, *Thanks, Dad, we really do need to know this . . . even if it is kinda embarrassing.*

When one of my daughters asked me, "Dad, don't you think sex is gross?" here's what I said.

"Let me ask you a question, honey. Can you trust Daddy?"

"Yes."

"Have I ever lied to you?"

"No," she said.

"Then you know that what I'm about to tell you is the truth. The day will come when the thought of having sex with a man—your husband—is going to sound very good to you. Yeah, I know it sounds gross now, but that day will come. I guarantee it."

> When my daughters were younger, the last words they wanted to hear out of my mouth were *sex*, *penis*, or *vagina*.

Because I am a man of faith, and I know too well from the multitudes of those I've counseled about the consequences of sex outside of marriage, I also introduced sex to my daughters in its spiritual context of two people becoming one.

"God created sex to be something wonderful between a husband and a wife," I continued, "but the world out there makes it sound nasty and dirty. There are all sorts of ways that people misuse it and demean women, but that's not how God originally designed it. He said that the husband and wife will become one,[1] and sex is one of the ways that two people who are committed to each other for a lifetime come together."

My daughter popped in with a question. "Why does everybody talk about it so much?"

"Because sex feels very good. Have you noticed how some parts of your body feel very nice when they are touched? Doesn't it feel special to get a back rub from Mom or Dad?"

"Yeah," she replied thoughtfully.

"Well, sex is like that, only more so."

What did I do in that conversation? I provided my daughter with a healthy introduction into the world of sexuality. She was talking to me, her father, a man she trusts and who is committed to never violating that trust. Even more, she heard about it in the context of the values of our family and my faith—as two becoming one—and I emphasized that sex is something reserved for marriage.

Every little girl deserves that kind of a conversation, and only her father can share that with her.

Don't rely on anyone else. Let it come from you.

Daddy-Daughter Movie Night

If you haven't seen the classic 1989 movie *Uncle Buck*, it's a great daddy-daughter movie, even though John Candy is the uncle who steps in and makes a difference in a rebellious teenage daughter's life. It kicked off some great discussion with my four daughters—ages ten, eleven, fourteen, and sixteen—when we watched it together, especially when I made this cryptic comment: "If a boy treated my daughter the way 'Bug' treated Tia, I think I'd do more than wave a hatchet in his direction. A significant body part might go missing." That got us all laughing and talking. I think in that one night we covered

more ground about sex and boys, with all four kids avidly listening and chiming in with their questions, than we ever had
before. Because of that movie, we talked about premarital sex,
what boys want (that's obvious), why a lot of girls give it to
them (acceptance, love), why some guys struggle with marriage (a fear of commitment), why girls put up with guys who
won't commit (they think the guy will change), and why the
teenager Tia dissed her parents and how that was resolved
through a major shift in attitude because of her experiences.
Our movie night was so successful that I'm already looking for
another classic we could all watch together. Got any ideas?

—Jeff, Texas

Kicking Off Discussions

You're at a nearby horse stable with your eight-year-old
daughter, and all of a sudden the stallion in the pasture gets more
than a little frisky with the mare. What do you do? Distract your
daughter? Cover her eyes? Or simply let her watch and ask questions as she's curious?

The best thing you can do with your daughter is answer the
questions she brings up in a straightforward manner. If she stops
asking questions, she's satisfied. If she asks more, she wants to
know more. Then you answer more. It's a simple plan, and it
works.

There's no need to shuffle your feet uncomfortably. Sex is a
part of life. Without it, your daughter wouldn't be on this planet.

"Dad, what are those horses doing?" your daughter asks.

"Well, one is a daddy horse and one is a mommy horse," you
begin. "They're working on making a baby horse."

Many eight-year-olds will stop there and simply watch what happens in nature, but if yours continues to ask questions, answer her in a steady, even tone, without embarrassment. And only answer the questions she asks. Then you don't have to wonder, *How far should I go here? Is this it? The big bazumba?*

One of the best places to talk with your daughter about sex and relationships is in the car. Perhaps you're on your way to that horse stable, or maybe your daughter is a figure skater or plays volleyball and you're on your way to a practice. There's nothing better than being able to stare straight ahead, concentrating on your driving, of course, as you talk to your daughter about growing up.

"I realized recently that you and I haven't had an opportunity to talk much about life. I've noticed that you're getting big—growing up awfully fast. Before long, those boys you think are pretty yucky are probably going to start looking good to you. Some guy will come around and show an interest in you and, all of a sudden, you'll have this feeling, *Wow, he's cute. I think he likes me.* You'll talk to your girlfriends about him. It's what your mom and I did when we were young. Your uncle and aunt and older cousin did too. It's a part of life. You'll have these feelings . . . almost euphoric.

> One of the best places to talk with your daughter about sex and relationships is in the car.

Some people call it 'puppy love,' but it's made of real feelings. That young boy and his interest will make you feel special . . ."

At that point in your talk, you can go a lot of different directions, based on the age of your daughter and the experiences she's had and your family has had. For example, if you have a relative who became pregnant out of wedlock at a young age, you can use that gently as an example: "We all make choices in life. Some are great ones, and others are not so good. Sometimes a teenager can change the entire course of his or her life by trying to grow up too fast and get involved with things they know are wrong or should be saved for later in life, in the right context."

If your daughter has been sexually abused in any way, this is the time to say straight out that the sexual abuse (by her uncle, a stepdad, whomever) was not her fault, and it does not make her dirty or "used material." It will also be important for your daughter to talk not just once, but multiple times along the way as she matures, to a trusted adult or professional counselor who can understand her thoughts and emotions and assist in guiding her to healthy relationships.

If you haven't talked to your daughter about boys and relationships before now, and she's already thirteen and boy-crazy, then you've got to up the ante a little more and take the discussion in a stronger direction. "I've noticed that you have a lot of interest in boys right now. And I'd be absolutely shocked if you didn't think some boys are cuter than others. A girl being attracted to boys is a natural thing . . ."

The best way to deal with a boy-crazy teenage daughter is to keep your eyes and ears open for which boy she's currently interested in, and, above all, don't make that boy the enemy. If you do, there will be another enemy around the corner—your daughter. Make your interactions as calm and natural as you can (yes, even if you're boiling inside at the way you see that boy treat your daughter). The one good thing is that teen relationships change more often than you think to change your boxers. So you can hold out the distinct hope that this will be one of them that goes the way of the dodo bird.

If your daughter is fourteen, and excited about soon being able to drive, say something like, "Honey, I can hardly believe you've only got four years left in this house under our wings.

I'm looking forward to some really great years. The time is soon going to come when you'll be out driving a car, enjoying a lot of the freedoms of living in this house. We want to be your partners as you grow up, not the heavies. What we will ask is that you meet our basic guidelines for coming home at a reasonable hour and for being careful who you hang out with and respectful of yourself and others on dates."

The most important thing of all is that your talks with your daughter are flavored with an air of confidence—that you believe in your daughter and know that she will make good decisions about everything in life, including boys. Having positive expectations of your daughter will go much further in your relationship than you can imagine.

> The best way to deal with a boy-crazy teenage daughter is to keep your eyes and ears open for which boy she's currently interested in, and, above all, don't make that boy the enemy.

Handling Physical Changes

I can't tell you how often a woman has told me she's had a conversation with her husband that went something like this:

> **DAD:** Uh, honey, I noticed that Amy is . . . you know, developing.
> **MOM:** Developing?
> **DAD:** Yeah, she's getting, well, I mean . . .
> **MOM:** Breasts. They're called breasts. She's thirteen years old. That's perfectly normal.

But from that point on, Dad awkwardly hugs his daughter because she's no longer a little girl, and those breasts are a reminder that things are obviously changing.

One of the worst things a father can do is pull back from his physically developing daughter, because that is the time when she's wondering most how males will view her as a woman. If her daddy draws away from her, it will confirm her worst fear: *I'm not beautiful enough to be loved.* Too many girls spend their adolescent years trying to lose weight so they look like the airbrushed magazine cover models, changing their hair and spending a fortune on makeup and clothes, to be "acceptable." Some fall into anorexia and bulimia. Many fall into the arms of hormone-driven boys, who gladly pay attention to them and give them emotional comfort . . . for a short while.

> Think back to when you were a teenager. How much did it take for you to get sexually excited?

If your daughter is in those hormone years, it's critically important that you affirm her as a young woman. Even something as simple as, "Hey"—and you whistle in admiration—"you look great in that outfit. Bet you're going to turn a few boys' heads today" might bring an outburst of, "Da-a-a-a-d!" But secretly she'll be thrilled you noticed and her budding womanhood will be affirmed.

Revealing What Boys Are Thinking

Think back to when you were a teenager. How much did it take for you to get sexually excited? Your daughter needs to know that it doesn't take much to get a thirteen-year-old boy, or a twenty-two-year-old boy for that matter, sexually excited. And a sexually excited boy can get more aggressive than a girl would expect. The majority of them will keep going, until they are told, quite firmly, to stop. In this world of instant information and specific language, don't wander around the subject. Address it head-on.

"If you sit in a boy's lap, he feels sexually stimulated," I told my daughter.

"No! Are you serious? Just sitting in his lap?"

"That's right. That's all it takes."

It also doesn't take a psychologist like me to figure out what can happen if a young man and woman go to see an R-rated movie or attend a dance and then hang out for two hours in a parked car. So I didn't let my daughters get into that situation. Instead, I told my daughters, "Sure, honey, you can spend time with Michael. Bring him over, and we'll all watch a movie or play a game together." Anything we could do in a context to keep my daughter out of the way of raging hormones.

Some of you may think I'm too protective. But, honestly, would you have allowed your two-year-old daughter to put her finger in an electrical outlet just to see what would happen? The ante is upped even more when hormones rage. So why would I allow my sixteen-year-old daughter, who has been dealing with boys for only a short while, to experience what it feels like to take her shirt off in the backseat of a car with an adolescent boy breathing down her neck and touching her breasts?

If you have an adolescent daughter, it's time to stand firm. The statistics for premarital sex are appalling. Do everything in your power to protect your daughter from becoming sexually active before marriage. The consequences—venereal diseases, a broken heart, intimacy problems, pregnancy outside marriage— are too severe for you not to take this one seriously.

The ace you hold is your involvement, Dad. Be affirming, loving, and open to all and any questions your daughter has about boys and sex. There's no such thing as having "the Talk" once and then it's over. Learning about the opposite sex is part of an ongoing relationship with you.

The Three Basic Questions of a Male Mind

1. Can I play with it?
2. Can I eat it?
3. Can I mate with it?

None of the above? Not interested.

Telling Stories

All kids love stories. It doesn't matter their age. And they love hearing them over and over. Tell your daughter stories about when you were dating.

Luke told his three daughters about the bumbling fool he made of himself when he forgot to walk the girl up to the door, and her dad told him in a heated tone, "You always walk girls up to the door. You don't leave them on the curb. Ever."

Miguel loves to tell his two kids about his first date with their mom. He arrived at her door. She opened it, looking beautiful in a dress and heels, shut it, and then opened it again.

"I didn't know you'd be so short," she said. "Just a minute, and I'll go change my shoes."

She left him standing again on her front porch with the door slammed shut and his mouth jammed open. A year later, they married. She wore flat shoes and still does to this day because she doesn't want to be taller than him.

When I asked Sande to marry me, I did so many things wrong it's a wonder we ever got together. Nobody told me I should take her to a nice place to propose. I took her to a field out behind my parents' house. After I popped the question and she agreed, I put the ring on the wrong hand. At city hall I told Sande it was a Leman tradition for the bride to pay for the wedding license.

"Oh, how interesting," she said sweetly. "I certainly don't want to break a Leman family tradition."

It was only after she coughed up the five dollars that I admitted she had just started the tradition because I'd neglected to bring the five bucks. Hey, I am the baby of the family, and I was so caught up in the exhilarating thought that this beautiful young woman was willing to live with me for the rest of her life that the details never occurred to me. It also never dawned on me, until much later—when Krissy's boyfriend, Dennis, asked me for her hand—that Sande's father was probably thinking, *This guy, who's only a janitor at the hospital, mopping up floors, is taking my daughter away?*

Every time you tell stories about your own dating years, you provide a sense of humor and perspective for when things go wrong on your daughter's dates. Like the time your daughter's skirt had a rip, and she had no idea she was flashing more of her backside than she intended until the end of her double date when the other girl finally risked telling her in the bathroom. Then she was mortified "before the whole world," as she'd put it. But whom did she call to come get her as she hid behind the plant at the restaurant? You, Dad.

When you reveal yourself as compassionate and open-minded, someone always safe to talk to, you'll win your daughter's heart and her trust.

Modeling a Healthy Sexuality

I don't apologize for liking sex, even at my age of near decrepitude. I think God's creativity hit a grand slam on that one. So I want my daughters to enjoy that same experience, provided it's within marriage. That's why I take my responsibility seriously to model a healthy, affirming attitude toward sexuality in my own marriage.

> I don't apologize for liking sex, even at my age of near decrepitude. I think God's creativity hit a grand slam on that one.

When my wife and I were taking two of our daughters through a book that helped to explain some of the facts of life, one of our daughters blurted out, "That's so gross."

"What is, honey?" Sande asked.

"Being naked under the covers."

The illustrations were chastely drawn but made it clear that mommy and daddy weren't wearing clothes.

"Well, how do you think you got here?" I asked her.

Suddenly, a light went on in my precious daughter's head—first the glimmer of understanding, then the fire of sheer indignation. "You mean you and Mommy get naked under the covers?"

"Yes, we do," I said.

This was followed by a Sherlock Holmes *aha.* "So that's why you lock your door on Saturday mornings. And I thought you just wanted to be nice to us when you let us watch cartoons!"

Our cover was blown. Actually, it was amazing it had lasted as long as it did. When Kevin and Krissy were very little, I frequently shushed them downstairs, told them to watch whatever they wanted, and explained that Mommy and Daddy needed to "talk."

They would leave, and I would bolt the door in four places and get under the covers with Sande. Within minutes, Kevin and Krissy would be back at the door. "Daddy? Are you in there? We can't hear you talking. I thought you said you and Mommy needed to talk."

"Get away from that door!" I would yell in the tone only a

father can use, and those tiny feet would scamper away faster than if they'd seen a monster.

But little kids often have short attention spans. Once, at what had to be absolutely the worst timing of their lives, Krissy and Kevin knocked on the door yet again. By this time I was living on another planet, and I couldn't even remember whether I had children, much less what their names were. So, great psychologist that I was, I pleaded with Sande, "Let's not say anything, and maybe they'll go away."

Sande gave me "the Look." The one that said, "I sacrificed for thirteen years past college to get you through your doctorate, and you come up with that?"

Finally, we heard Krissy say to her brother, "Kevey, looks like you better go get the hammer. I think they may need our help."

With those words I crashed back into Earth's atmosphere. Incidents such as those help to explain why many an audience since has heard me mutter, "We have seen the enemy, and they are small—and unionized."

While very young kids can make intimacy difficult, a daughter deserves a father who is crazy about his wife. A daughter also needs a mother who welcomes her husband's advances. So if you're a married man, hug your wife and give her a passionate kiss in front of the kids. When you do, your daughter will never go to sleep wondering if her parents will get a divorce. She'll know she is loved and secure.

The Building Blocks of a Healthy Relationship with the Opposite Sex

In talking with young children about sex and the male perspective, one of the most profound things I ever shared with a group is, "Start with the head and work your way down."

What do young girls like? My granddaughter, Adeline, is seven as I write this book. She loves to take the makeup her grandma gives her, sit in people's laps, and do everybody's makeup in the room. Appearance is important to her already, even at age seven. Contrast that to boys at age seven, who have to be cajoled to comb their hair or take a bath.

So talk to your daughter about the building blocks for a successful relationship with the opposite sex.

Appearance

God Almighty has given all of us certain looks. But it's up to us what we decide to do with them. How we appear to others is often how we're thought of, and it can greatly influence the kinds of relationships we get involved in. How else do you explain the teenage daughter with a nose ring, belly ring, and three ear piercings who, when she goes on her second round of job interviews, all of a sudden more closely resembles Pollyanna in her dress? The person you appear to be will attract a certain clientele. Nothing makes me more sad as a father than watching young women reveal way too much of themselves in a desperate attempt to attract the opposite gender. I want to grasp the arm of each of them and say, "You are more valuable than that. Don't sell yourself short."

Boys will look. They will always look. They're engineered to look at, and greatly appreciate, the female anatomy. What your daughter needs to know is that boys will always be intrigued by the mystery of a woman. But if she reveals all, the mystery is gone.

So slip your daughter a commercial announcement. "Honey, I gotta hand it to you. You always look nice. You take good care of yourself. I'm a guy, and I don't know much about makeup and color combinations, but every time I see you, I say, 'Wow, now there's a girl who thinks enough of herself to always be neat, clean, and dress attractively.'"

Your daughter might not respond to your encouragement on the spot, but I guarantee she'll be smiling all over for hours. *My dad notices me. He sees the effort I put in to look good.*

Slip your daughter a commercial announcement.

Even young girls like my grandchild Adeline will spend hours in front of a mirror, literally sitting in the washbowl in the bathroom. They'll play with their hair, experiment with different lipsticks, try on all sorts of facial expressions. It's all a part of a girl's growing up.

No wonder you can barely get in the bathroom if you have a daughter.

The best thing you can do for yourself is build another bathroom—at least a small one that has a toilet and a sink.

Good luck, Dad.

Poise

How your daughter carries herself on a daily basis says everything about how she feels about herself. Does she walk with her eyes on the ground, shoulders slumped? Then she has a low self-worth. If she faces the world with a smile and a quick step, and focuses straight ahead on the challenges of the day, she's confident in who she is. This poise and confidence comes from you, Dad. Any daughter who knows she's loved by her daddy, supported by her daddy, and protected by her daddy has a great start in the world.

There's another very important side benefit to poise, as well. The Heidi Search Center, which helps both to track and find missing children and to inform parents, says, "You must take an active interest in your children. Listen to them, love them unconditionally and help build their self-esteem." Why is this so important? Because child molesters look for children who aren't assertive and confident, the Heidi Search Center says. That's why they suggest, "Make your home a place of trust and support that meets your child's needs. . . . Children can be raised to be friendly and polite, but assertive. CHILDREN HAVE THE RIGHT TO SAY NO. If anyone asks them to do things that make them uncomfortable, they can say NO. Teach them to TRUST their instincts. If something feels wrong, it probably is. SAY NO!"[2]

Understanding

Boys clearly are different from girls. Your role, Dad, is to take advantage of natural situations that come along in life to provide teachable moments.

For example, your eleven-year-old daughter says to you, "Boys are so dumb sometimes." She jams a thumb toward her two brothers, who have gone from flexing their muscles at each other to wrestling on the front lawn, all to show off for the cute girl who's new in the neighborhood.

You laugh. "I agree with you there. They are dumb. They're even dumber when they think that doing that will impress Heather. They haven't figured out how to relate to girls yet, have they? You'd rather a boy talked to you than wrestled you, right?"

You've planted a seed, Dad.

Your seven-year-old daughter is walking along the street with you when you see a cluster of boys around a teenage girl whose T-shirt is low enough that her personal items might pop out and say hello any minute. "Wow," you say quietly to your daughter as you hold her hand, "that girl sure doesn't think she's worth much."

"Why, Dad?" your daughter asks, puzzled.

"The way she's dressed tells me the only way she thinks she can get a boy's attention is by showing more of her skin than she should. The boys she'll attract aren't the kind of boys who will take care of her."

You've planted a message that your daughter will think about later, as she's choosing her own clothing in her teen years.

Mutual Respect

Without mutual respect, there can be no relationship. Mutual respect means that you don't put down the other gender whether in thought or in talk. Men and women are different. Neither is better or worse; they're merely different.

Dad, your daughter needs to know that you care. She'll listen to your life lessons only if you're not preaching, if you don't act like you have all of life's lessons in your back pocket, and if she knows you're in her corner as her champion.

"Honey, I believe in you, and I want you to have the greatest teenage years anyone's ever had . . ."

> She'll listen to your life lessons . . . only if she knows you're in her corner.

Understand that kids will always be kids. Your daughter will roll her eyes, stomp her feet, and slam doors every once in a while. Don't go looking for trouble. Take the edge out of the air with a little humor whenever you can. And set the stage for forgiveness by approaching her first when you've been out of line.

"Honey, I apologize for snapping at you this morning. As soon as I did that, I told myself, *Sheesh, I really need to work on my temper.* And I am working on it. In fact, I asked your mom to help me with that. I'm asking for your help too."

The reality is that you have all the gold in your back pocket.

Your daughter wouldn't even be wearing that training bra if you didn't buy it for her. You're the parent; you have everything. But when you show respect for your daughter not only as a member of your family but also as a female, you're setting her up to look for relationships with other boys and men who will also show her respect.

I've got news for you. Today teenage girls can do anything they want to do. It's not hard to find drugs these days. It's not hard to get sex. Who's kidding who? The temptation to do things that can have long-term consequences is huge during those critical years. Other kids will tell your daughter, "Hey, smoke this, snort that. Come to the party on Friday night." Your daughter is the one who is going to have to make those decisions. You aren't always going to be walking around with her, snowplowing the roads of life for her.

Your job as a dad is to make sure your daughter feels special and secure, since those are the two keys to her making good choices.

Long-Term Perspective

Dads always ask me where they should draw the line regarding sexual boundaries with their daughters. I'd love to be able to give you the perfect recipe, but that's how husbands get in trouble with wives—thinking they need a recipe for sex. You need this and this and this, and then this happens. But life isn't like that. Providing healthy boundaries is about a relationship. Believe it or not, we Lemans never had a curfew for our five kids when they were teenagers. We simply said, "Come home at a reasonable hour."

Our kids didn't like it. They would rather we said, "Come home by 11:15 p.m., or we'll whack you with a magic wand and turn you into a pumpkin."

Instead, we had positive expectations of them. We had reared our kids to be responsible and courteous of others, and we never had a single problem with any of them. If you allow your daughter to drive a car, you'd better think she's responsible. If she isn't, why are you allowing her to have in her hands a tool that could seriously injure or kill herself and others?

Each family's boundaries will be different for dating, and they need to be discussed up front with respect. I believe that you have preliminary discussions much earlier than the age at which your daughter might start dating. Sometimes incidents in school are natural ways to launch discussions. For example, someone says something improper, inappropriately touches your daughter, or makes fun of her body. Take advantage of those situations to talk about mutual respect, how you treat others, and how you expect others to treat you.

For example, a conversation might go something like this:

"The time is going to come when a boy will try something with you that you feel is inappropriate or that you know goes against our family values. When that happens, what will you say? What will you do about it? I want to make sure you have some tools to deal with it when it does happen."

> Each family's boundaries will be different for dating, and they need to be discussed up front with respect.

Then you go on to share some personal experiences from your own dating years, where you had to address uncomfortable situations and thoughts. What made you pull back from going too far on a date? What little voice inside told you, *No, I don't want to go there. We need to stop now*?

A general conversation such as this is also helpful:

"Boys by their nature have the ability to be blinded by what's on the outside. So I'm going to tell you something not only because I'm your dad and want to protect you, but because I know you're attractive, and other boys will think so too. They'll find you attractive, like I found your mom attractive.

"I met your mom when I was eighteen, only five years older than you are now. It didn't take me long to fall in love with her. I wanted to spend every waking moment with her. Talk about warm feelings and wanting to be close—wow! But one of the reasons we've been married seventeen years, and we're looking forward to being married forever, is that we developed our relationship based on mutual understanding, respect, and love. We knew, with the way we felt about each other, that things could get steamy. We didn't want to fall into doing things that we knew could hurt us or our relationship later. So we built in some parameters to protect ourselves. Every young person has to do that, and you will too. Many parents think they can issue edicts—you'll go this far, and no farther, and they slash a line of anything from the neck down—and that those edicts become practice in their kids' lives.

"But I'm not that stupid. I know that what you do on dates is a decision that you have to make, because you are the one who will deal with the results for the rest of your life. Since you've been little, we've given you chores to do around the house. That's not because we're lazy and want someone else to do it. No, it's an opportunity for you to learn to be responsible—for your room, for a certain activity, and for your life in general. The time will come when you leave our nest. You'll be on your own. We'll celebrate your achievements, and we'll always want what's best for you. But we won't be in charge of your life. You will. We want you to have the absolute best life you can. I believe in you. I'm confident you will make good choices."

Dad, the stakes are high. Take advantage of life's teachable moments and natural situations. Talk to your daughter about the important things of life—such as sex, dating, and boys—before they occur. If you haven't yet and she's already in the dating zone, don't wait another day. Who better than you to slip your daughter some commercial announcements about the basic building blocks for successful relationships with the opposite sex?

Ask Dr. Leman: How Honest Should I Be?

Q: I first had sex when I was fifteen. The girl I was with was fourteen. I hadn't planned on it going that far, but it did. Afterwards, I could never look at that girl the same way, and I broke up with her. We'd been dating only two months. I wish I'd known then what I know now—that sex changes things in a relationship. My daughter will be fourteen next month, and boys are eyeing her. Because of what I did, how can I tell her not to have sex? That she'll wish she hadn't? It still bothers me to this day how I treated that girl. She was a nice girl and deserved to be treated better. I'd hate to think somebody would treat my daughter that way.

—Marcus, Maine

A: You should talk with your daughter *because* you had that experience. You don't need to give her specifics, but you do need to be honest. Tell her that when you were dating, you didn't treat girls the way you should have and it bothers you to this day. Tell her that the first girl you went out with was a really nice girl who deserved better. "In fact," you can say, "that's why I'm talking to you now. I don't ever want you to be in the place where you let some guy take advantage of you because you think you should just because you're on a date, everybody does it, or you think you don't deserve better . . ." Go on to tell her what's special about her, what you think of her and her worth, and that you know she's got a bright future ahead, complete with a wonderful man who will love her for her. Conclude with, "And if you're ever in a situation where you're not comfortable, call me. I'll come and get you, no questions asked."

Advice About Sex Within Marriage— and What Men Really Want

Sadly, far too many women have shared with me in counseling what their mothers told them on their wedding day: "Sex is something you're going to have to learn to live with. Lie back and let him enjoy himself." What a terrible view of the most thrilling, intimate moment that God Almighty created between a man and a woman who have committed to each other for a lifetime! If your wife grew up with this view of sex, it's no wonder that gardening is far more important to her or she finds dishes to do when you're giving her that Bullwinkle look.

It's critically important that you convey to your daughter how wonderful sex can be—in the right context of marriage. Fulfilling sex isn't merely "going through the motions because a man needs it." Sex without sexual fulfillment to a man is like conversing with a man through a newspaper to a woman. She might seek conversation, but not when it's like that.

When we choose marriage, we must choose to put the needs of our partner before our own needs. As your daughter enters her dating years and begins thinking about a lifetime partner, she needs to know how important sex is to a man, understand that, and go out of her way to provide exciting experiences within the marriage relationship.

If you're a woman reading this chapter, you're saying to yourself, "Sex will never be that exciting to me. I don't get it. I'd rather cuddle." But that's exactly why I'm encouraging fathers to teach their daughters to put their marriage partner first. If you want your man to be content in marriage and satisfied with you, then you want him to drive to work smiling, thinking, *I'm so glad I married that woman. I've got to be the luckiest guy on the planet.* That man would take a bullet for you. He'll clean up the kids' vomit and do dishes. He'll stand up for you against the bully neighbor.

In the same way, men, your first inclination isn't to arrive home from work and to enjoy a half-hour conversation with your wife about your day. All you want is a shower followed by a brain rinse of flipping channels with the remote control. But because you love your wife, you choose her needs first, and you talk with her.

Most of the couples who have entered my counseling office suffer from the same disease: selfishness. The wife refuses to initiate more sexually because the husband isn't romantic enough. The husband says he can't think romantically if he doesn't get enough sex. If they continue on that path, the result will be a divorce. However, if both are willing to put each other first, that marriage can not only become revitalized but more exciting and passionate than they could ever dream.

If you want your daughter to have that kind of a lifetime relationship, you need to tell her the truth. Sex matters—greatly—to a guy. But even more important than the sex to her man is how enthusiastically the one he loves enters into that part of the marriage relationship.

What Men Need Most

- To be wanted
- To be needed
- To be fulfilled/respected

What Women Need Most

- Affection
- Honest, open communication
- Commitment to family

For Dads with Divided Loyalties

In today's society, where so many young people have experienced sex in some form, some of you dads had sex early in life. You got into situations you wish you hadn't, and that might still haunt you. For you, the ante is upped even further. What led you into those situations as a teenage boy? How did you view that girl you had sex with? What happened in your relationship after "the event"? For the majority of teens, relationships spiral downward after sex enters the picture. Breakups are rampant.

Do you really want your daughter to experience the breakup of a relationship? Especially after sex is involved? Breakups can be extremely devastating for five reasons, says the *Huffington Post*:

1. "Rejection is physiologically heart-breaking." It leads us to view ourselves as passive victims.
2. "We are hard-wired to fear rejection." Everyone wants approval and acceptance; breakups shut that down.
3. "Getting over a breakup is like getting over cocaine." We go through withdrawal.
4. "We aren't that good at dealing with loss." Our brains view loss as more significant than gain, so we don't want to take risks on other relationships.
5. "The more we fail, the more the goal seems insurmountable." The more rejection we receive, the less we try to find real love.[3]

Some of you have divided loyalties. You have a daughter with your ex, your stepdaughter lives with you, or you have a daughter with your second wife. A lot of stepdads do a great job as parents, but it is a different ball game. As I've said before, living in a blended family sometimes feels like being pureed in a blender without the lid on, with the results exploding all over the kitchen wall.

The best thing you can do is be honest with your daughter who isn't living with you: "Honey, if I could live life over again, which I can't, I'd be married once. I hate that you live in a different location than me and I can't see you every day. But life doesn't always go the way you want it to or that you dream it'll go. Your mom and I split, and there were a lot of hurts. For that, I'm very sorry. I never want you to have to choose between us, and I would never force you to do that. We can't erase the bad things that happened in the past, but we can choose to move forward. I know that might be difficult because I've caused you pain. But I am willing to try."

For dads who had sexual experiences before marriage and

had daughters out of wedlock, keep in mind that you are not under any obligation to divulge personal information to your kids. It's obvious that you had sex out of wedlock if your daughter is the result. She doesn't need to know any more than that. You need to be able to walk that fine line of teaching your daughter what's right with a good degree of wisdom. "Honey, I made some bad choices in life. But out of those bad choices came a wonderful gift—you. I wouldn't trade you for anything. However, I also don't want you to go through what your mom and I did . . ."

When Your Daughter Likes a Boy

When you hear your daughter using a boy's name over and over, hello, you don't have to have a PhD to know this person is a special guy to your daughter.

So what does the smart dad do?

"Hey, honey, you've mentioned this fellow Rob a bunch of times, and it sounds like you think he's pretty cool. I've never had the pleasure of meeting him. We're going to watch the ball game at seven o'clock, have pizza, and hang out a little. You're welcome to invite him over. Your call, not mine."

That's the way to keep the tennis ball on your daughter's side of the court. The danger is in trying to micromanage your daughter's life as she grows older and needs to begin to play life's game by herself. What you can do well is teach responsibility, integrity, compassion, and respect from the time she's young.

By the way, it's no fair brandishing a firearm when Rob walks into the room. That might work in movies, but in real life, it's too much. However, a firm handshake would be a good option. Realize that your daughter is going to be a little nervous if she accepts your gracious offer, but keep in mind that if she takes you up on that offer, she must believe in you and your ability to handle the situation, and that says volumes about the relationship you've built with her.

If she does bring Rob around, the benefit is you get to meet this fella who is vying for your daughter's attention. Have fun . . . and make sure you take your blood pressure medicine.

Remember, it's all about the relationship. Yours and your daughter's.

Dads who are there for their daughters increase their daughters' success in every walk of life.

A Good Dad's Quick Reference Guide

- Tell stories.
- Build your relationship.

SIX

Help! Civil War Just Broke Out in the Family Room

What to do when the females in your house are at war and you're waving the truce flag.

When I was young, we used to play a game called "Pickle in the Middle." Two or more players had to pass a ball to each other—if there were more players, they stood in a circle—while the player in the middle tried to intercept it. Being the guy in the middle was a tough place to be, since the other players were trying hard to exclude you. And if you're the youngest child in your family, like me, you have vivid memories of riding in the back or middle seat of the car. To this day, I hate being sandwiched in the middle seat of an airplane. You'll always find me in the first row or one back, in an aisle seat.

There's nothing more miserable than being a dad caught in the middle between two females in your family, with the warfare turning your home into chaos. You'd take a bullet for either of them, but now you're asked to choose. The result is a big mess that oozes everywhere, like a steadily spreading oil slick.

Daughter Warfare

If you have daughters, you already know the definition of *catfight* and also that World War III can occur if one of them wears the other's clothing. Well, as a dad, I got sick of the bickering:

"You left my sweater in a heap."

"You didn't hang up my skirt."

"There's a dirty spot on it."

"Dad! She . . ."

"Mom! She . . ."

> Whoever invented the word *catfight* must have had sisters or daughters.

So I decided to be king and issue a royal edict. "You are *not* wearing each other's clothes—ever."

It was hard for them to have any comeback with such a straightforward statement. And that's one thing we dads are good at, let me tell you.

Anytime you take a stand, you will get your daughters' attention. When they are fighting, they know exactly what they're doing. They've played this game before, and their antics are designed to draw you, Dad, into their battles. But here are my top tips to handling these squabbles and keeping your manliness intact.

Tip #1: Don't Walk into Those Traps

Fighting is an act of cooperation. It takes two to tango, and your daughters are really good at it. In fact, they're masters at fighting with each other and manipulating you.

When boys have problems, they'll shout it out and wrestle, and the issue will be resolved swiftly. It's a well-known fact that boys don't use as many words as girls do. Girls can go after each other verbally for a very long time. Whoever invented the word *catfight* must have had sisters or daughters.

Tip #2: Express Your Fatherly Disapproval for Events That Happen Continuously

Say, "You know, this is getting a little old." You point each daughter to her room, or separate rooms if they share a bedroom. "I think both of you need time to think about this. For the record, Mom and I really don't appreciate hearing the bickering. In fact, I'm pretty disappointed in what's going on in this house right now."

Jared, who had always been a permissive dad, was so tired of his three stair-step daughters fighting that he finally said to them one night, "I've been sitting here trying to watch TV, but the whole time I've been distracted by the three of you and the disgusting way you talk to each other. You guys are old enough to figure this out once and for all. So I'm giving you five minutes to go out of this room and settle it peacefully without screaming and name-calling. Here's my promise to you: If you don't solve it in the next five minutes, I'll solve it for you. And if I solve it for you, I can guarantee none of you will like it."

Silence descended upon that living room. Because Jared had always been a pushover dad who let his wife handle things, his daughters weren't sure whether to take him seriously or not. Five minutes later, when the name-calling continued, Jared solved the problem. He was right. None of the girls liked it . . . especially when they saw he was serious and his decision removed all social networking devices from his home for a month—an eternity for three adolescent girls.

But after that, Jared was able to watch his program in silence, and his three girls became much more respectful of one another and their dad. All it took was a few well-delivered words in a steady tone by the father to make a difference.

Because the cross-gender relationship between daddy and daughter is so important, it makes a huge impact when you express that you're not a happy camper. Even if your daughters don't seem to be paying attention, believe me, they are.

Tip #3: Stand Firm on the Fact That Nothing Happens Until the Fight Is Resolved

That means one daughter doesn't go to her basketball game; the other doesn't go to a friend's house. They work the issue out first. When the fight doesn't gain either of them anything and it puts a crimp in their plans, they won't be tempted to continue it . . . and they'll think a little harder about the consequences before they start the next fight.

Tip #4: Butt Out

Leave the two fighters alone to solve the problem. It's amazing how swiftly and creatively problems can get resolved when there isn't an audience.

More than anything, your daughters want to please you. That's their inner motivation. When they know you're not happy and that they're causing your unhappiness, you're in the driver's seat to see change happen—for the good.

Stuck in the Middle?

- Be pragmatic and unemotional.
- Use only a few words.
- Deliver a to-the-point message.

Dads who remember these things when in the heat of battle between females will come out feeling good about themselves.

When Mama and Daughter Are Going at It

When the females in your house are waging war, what happens next has everything to do with how you respond.

If you're a hothead and you fly off the handle, saying things such as, "Would you two cut it out? I'm sick of hearing it" and "Stop it. Stop it right now. You two are acting like idiots," you're just pushing the warfare tactics to a higher level. But if you have a calm demeanor in the midst of battle, you can be an emotionally settling force in your family.

There's some important information you need to know first, and it's about Mama. Mama Bear is most likely to knock heads with the daughter who is most like her. So if you've ever mumbled to yourself (out of your wife's hearing, of course), "These two deserve each other," you're spot on. But like a dad can be a good teacher to a daughter, he can also be a great teacher to a wife.

Listen carefully, though. You *never* do this in front of a daughter. You always do it behind closed doors, where only you and your wife are involved in the conversation.

You might say something like this: "Honey, you're the queen of relationships, and far be it from me to even suggest you do things differently. But it seems to me that this whole thing—the big hassle we've had in our home—started when you greeted Little Missy at breakfast with not a hello or a good morning but a 'Have you cleaned the bathroom yet?' I know as a man that I hate it when people ask me questions. I think maybe things got off on the wrong foot this morning and sort of spiraled down . . ."

This is where you, Dad, need to be the pragmatic one in the family. Don't get dragged into the fight. Stay out of it emotionally.

Even when your wife snips back with, "If you're asking me to apologize, I'm *not* going to," you stay steady.

You say calmly, "You do what you think is best. But if you do come to that decision at some point, I think you'd be showing her how big of a person you can really be." Then extend the olive branch to your wife and say something like, "How do you feel right now? Good about your relationship with her?"

Most women will then calm down and say, "Well, no, I don't."

Then gently add, "I'm not the relationship expert you are, and I could be wrong, but I think you need to own up to your part of it." You might even want to add a little bit of humor: "Maybe part of the problem is that you're both wired pretty similarly."

But when push comes to shove, and your manhood and everything else is at stake, if you have to choose between your girls, you'd better run with Mama.

I've never met a wife who told me, "I'm so thankful that I'm number two in my husband's heart, and his children are number one."

Your first priority has to be your wife—for your sake, her sake, and your daughter's sake.

No Longer Ground Zero in My House

My wife and first daughter have always had a difficult relationship. I first saw it when Kendra was three, and I came home and found them glaring into each other's faces. Neither would move; neither was willing to give in. When Kendra turned thirteen, the yelling got so bad between them that several times after arriving home from work, I got back in the car and drove back to work. I know that sounds terrible, but I was sick of all the drama. One of those nights a coworker found me slumped over my desk with my head in my hands and asked me what was up. When I explained, he smiled knowingly.

"Sounds like my house before we all read a book," he said.

That book was *The Birth Order Book,* and he let me borrow the copy he had in his desk. I sat at work that night and read the entire thing in one sitting. I finally realized why my wife and first daughter fought so much—they were both firstborns and determined to win. Neither ever backed down. I was a middle-born and tired of playing peacemaker between them.

I got home at eleven o'clock that night, and all was quiet. My wife and daughter were both asleep. I asked my boss the next day if I could have a longer than usual lunch hour and surprised my wife by taking her out to lunch at her favorite restaurant. We had a long discussion, based on parts of *The Birth Order Book* that I had flagged. I never once mentioned that I was doing it because I was sick of having Ground Zero in my house. My wife was so intrigued, she wanted to keep the book. By that night, she'd read the whole book cover to cover too.

"You know, Kendra might be interested in this too," she said. "Since we're not doing so well together, she probably wouldn't read it if I asked her. But if *you* asked her . . ."

So we agreed that I'd surprise Kendra by picking her up after school and taking her out to her favorite restaurant for an early dinner the next night. I had a similar conversation with her. She, too, was intrigued by what *The Birth Order Book* was saying. She started talking about how it would help her understand her friends at school.

"Oh, by the way, Dad," she said, "my friends cancelled on our Friday night movie. Maybe we could get some pizza and talk more about this?"

I quietly arranged for our other two younger children to be away that night during our discussion. I didn't want them in our house if Ground Zero hit again.

My wife, daughter, and I were talking about birth order as we munched pizza when, all of a sudden, my daughter smacked the table.

"So that's why!" she exclaimed. "I'm a firstborn. Mom's a firstborn. And it says right here that firstborns are groomed to win, no matter what it costs them in relationships. That's why we fight all the time . . ." She sneaked a glance at her mom. "Uh, sorry, Mom."

My wife's jaw dropped. She, too, realized what was going on.

Since that night, life hasn't always been smooth between the two of them. But our discussions that week were a distinct turning point in their relationship. Now about 95 percent of the time they give each other grace. The other 5 percent of the time they're learning to say, "I'm sorry." My younger son even said, "Wow, Dad, what did you do? Wave a magic wand or something? Mom and Kendra don't fuss anymore."

Well, that magic wand for our family was *The Birth Order Book*. Since then, we've all read a bunch more of your books, and they've helped us in lots of ways. Keep writing them! You've made a huge difference in our family.

—Matt, Connecticut

How Natural Changes Increase Competition

How your wife was raised by her father and her birth order in the family has everything to do with how she sees your daughter and you. What was your wife's relationship like with her dad? Warm? Affirming? Or did she always feel inferior? Was she treated distantly or like a princess?

If her father was critical (the subject of the next chapter), then she has told herself lies her entire life about how she's never good enough. She may look like she's doing great in life on the outside, but something inside clobbers her on the head even when she excels.

You may have married "Daddy's little princess," for whom the thinking that she can get whatever she wants is ingrained. She may use tears, feigned illnesses, or even tantrums to get her way, but she always does.

Did she have to do something big to be noticed? Maybe she was the rebel, who got her kicks out of disappointing her daddy . . . or the saint who was "perfect" because she didn't dare cross him.

If your wife is comfortable around men, that means she grew up around them and prefers their company because she's had a positive father-daughter experience. She'll also be more easily able to relate to you. But if she was an only child, she may have little understanding or patience with your daughters' sibling rivalry.

When your daughter was born, most likely you noticed that your wife had an uncanny sense of what babies need, and an amazing, almost intuitive understanding of what that baby was trying to communicate. You struggled to know the difference between a "hungry" cry and an "I'm wet" cry. Your wife just knew. But because Mama was so adept at anticipating her daughter's desires, your daughter may not learn how to communicate her needs effectively without her. When a father interacts with his baby, his daughter is forced to learn how to communicate in different ways so others can understand. So, Dad, your supposed "weakness" actually helps strengthen your daughter for the future. It's a good thing you don't parent like a woman!

When that baby becomes a toddler, you're needed again—to help your daughter learn how to accept a man's attention. Up to this point, your wife has been integrally connected to your child. After all, you can't breast-feed, can you? Enough said. As toddlers grow toward school age, a mom may feel jealous of her daughter's interest in spending time with her father. *I was the one who changed all those diapers and rocked her to sleep, and now she wants him more than me?* But a daughter's growing interest in a relationship with her father is a very good and necessary thing.

> Dad, your supposed "weakness" actually helps strengthen your daughter for the future.

It's normal for a five-year-old daughter to seek her father's attention and even resent her mother, especially if she views her mother as "taking time away" from her activities with her father. But such changes are critical in your daughter defining what being *feminine* means. If both you and your wife understand what's going on and talk about it, there will be less competition between your wife and your daughter for your attention. You also have the wonderful opportunity to show your daughter how Mom and Dad resolve conflict in healthy ways . . . together.

Between the ages of six and preadolescence, a daughter's view of her daddy will change from an idealized one ("My daddy is perfect—the biggest and the best") to a more realistic one ("My daddy has strengths and weaknesses, like everybody else"). At this stage, an involved father can help his daughter begin the necessary separation from Mama instead of regressing to being a baby again, where Mama calls all the shots. However, Dad, be aware that this stage can be extremely painful and hurtful for your wife, who may feel pushed away unless she truly understands what's going on. Her baby is growing up.

In adolescence, the involved father becomes the male figure that all other men are compared to. If you accept her, affirm her, and encourage her, she'll be able to successfully negotiate her way into adulthood. Mother and daughter can become "best friends" at this age, something every Mama longs for. However, Mama still needs to be careful that she doesn't guard their girl time together so possessively that their daughter is cheated from receiving Dad's all-important attention.

In every stage of life—from birth to marriage—an active father's presence is crucial. If both Mom and Dad understand the stages and why they're happening, life will flow much more smoothly in the household.

Yesterday, Luke, the dad of an only child who's a freshman in high school, told me how excited he is that his daughter will soon be able to get her driver's permit. "It's a great new stage in her growing independence. She's a wonderful, confident kid, and she'll be a terrific driver. It'll help my wife out a lot too—not having to drive her everywhere after she gets her license."

Contrast that to his wife's response: "Wow, our baby is growing up," she said a bit tearfully. "Sometimes I want to go back to those baby days, where I held her safely in my arms and rocked her to sleep."

See the difference? Dad, when you know those differences and understand the stages, you'll be able to navigate competently through the minefields of female relationships. Other dads, in fact, will be asking you for advice. Both mother and daughter need your attention, steadiness, wisdom, understanding, and unconditional love.

However, I want to be absolutely clear on this issue: the best gift you can give your daughter is making your wife number one in your eyes. You're not raising a healthy daughter if you shower all your attention on "Daddy's little girl" and leave nothing for Daddy's wife.

> The best gift you can give your daughter is making your wife number one in your eyes.

Some of you are divorced dads, and you winced at those words. But let's just say it: divorce is never cool, and lots of people pay. But you lessen the payment for your daughter if you

- don't dog your ex-wife about anything.
- affirm your love for your daughter.
- are involved in a positive way in her life.
- are quick to ask your daughter's opinion about things that relate to herself, you, and other members of the family.
- don't fall into the trap of over-giving things to her.
- remember that if you love her, you'll also discipline her.

If you do these few things, Dad, your daughter has a great shot of living a fulfilling life.

For those of you who are married, the woman you married always comes first. If you keep your wife as your priority, your daughter will see a healthy marriage with two cooperating partners and be able to develop an appropriate model for her own marriage someday.

If you want to be a successful father, be an active father and an active husband.

Max's teenage daughter, Beth, is normally quiet but can talk a blue streak when they're in the car. So he, being the smart dad he is, finds ways to get her on minitrips, even if it's to a drive-through for some hot chocolate for a study break.

One day Beth said, "I don't know what I want to do after college. But I do know what I don't want to do."

"And what's that?" Max said.

"Work."

Max couldn't help himself. He laughed. "You know, Bethie, working is part of this world."

"I know that. I'm willing to work, but I want to work like Mom—at home. I want to be a mom."

Ah, now was the time for a teachable moment, and Max knew it. "If you want to be like Mom, then you better marry someone like Dad—someone who is committed to the values of having the mother stay at home and raise the kids. Not every man will want that."

What was Max doing? Showing his now-interested-in-boys daughter that Mom and Dad work as a team. If Beth wants the life her mother enjoys, she'll need to pick a husband who is similar to her father.

Beth will be reflecting on that conversation for a long time—about the great role models she has of both mother and father. Together, her parents are helping her understand how a man and a woman relate, work together, and raise a healthy family.

Isn't that what you want for your daughter, Dad? For her to have the best chance for happiness in her own marriage? If so, learn to get along with your wife. Shower your daughter with affection, but save the primary flow of your attention for your wife. If you do this, your entire family will benefit.

A Good Dad's Quick Reference Guide

- Stay calm.
- Side with Mama.

SEVEN

The Critical Eye

What makes you good in the workplace can work against you at home. Here's how to turn things around.

I was sitting at a Bobbie Sox game (for those of you who don't know, that's girls' softball) on a beautiful sunny day when an eight-year-old blonde stepped up to the plate. The entire time she was batting, her father was yelling at her from the stands.

"Spread your feet wider. Put your hands together on the bat . . ."

I cringed for that little girl. Clearly, she was embarrassed and stressed. Who wouldn't be with that know-it-all dad? I shook my head. So much damage is done by dads who know how life ought to be for everyone else and end up vicariously living their lives through their children.

Simply stated, he was a knucklehead.

Many of us men think we know everything. We're groomed from babyhood to compete, so we're critical of those around us and don't even realize how harsh we're being on our daughters.

In the movie *A Walk in the Clouds,* a young woman arrives home at her family's vineyard in California. What her family doesn't know is that she's pregnant, and that a kind GI (Keanu Reeves) has agreed to pretend he's her husband in order to protect her, at least temporarily, from her controlling, critical-eyed father. When her father demands to know the truth, she says, "The only truth you want is the truth according to you." Along the way, Reeves falls in love with her, and pleads with her father, "Can't you see how special she is?" But the father continues to criticize her. When his domineering ways and wrath nearly destroy his own vineyard and thus his family's way of life for generations, he is brought to his knees. His family gathers around him, and he has to admit to his daughter, "I was afraid of losing you . . . all of you."[1]

You see, the critical-eyed person's need to control people and situations actually comes from a deep insecurity. The insecure person tries to make himself feel better by putting everyone else down. This insecurity comes with a mantra that says, "Life has to be perfect. There's a right way to do everything, and it's my way. I have all the answers, and I have to be right. That means I have to control the situation."

Critical-Eyed Dad Scenarios

Your daughter is ready to go out on a date. She comes down the stairs dressed in something you don't think is appropriate.

You bark, "You're not going out like that!"

And she screams, "Mother!"

"Your room looks like a pigsty. I'm sick of looking at it."

"But, Dad, I—"

"How many times do I have to tell you to keep your room clean?"

"Dad, I need money."

"What do you mean you need money? I gave you money last week."

"I spent that. It's all gone."

"What do you think—that money grows on trees? You are so irresponsible. I thought you could handle money better than that."

When the grades come home, your daughter has five As and one B+.

You say, "Hey, what's with the B+?"

Your daughter comes home, crushed because she didn't get the job she wanted.

You say, "Well, if you had worn something that looked more businesslike, you would have gotten it."

What Thumper's Mama Said Still Holds True

"If you can't say something nice,
don't say nothin' at all."[2]

Critical-eyed dads can find the flaw in anything. They're always taking the cheap shot, the hit that says, "You could do better." I see this in the stories of so many adults who tell me, "My parents never said, 'I'm proud of you' or 'I love you.'"

In addition, a lot of parents use their children. For example, I know a twenty-nine-year-old woman who is very good at math. She became her father's bookkeeper and office manager as soon as she graduated from college. Last Friday night, when she was ready to leave at 5:00 p.m., her father came in, frowned at her desk, and said, "Listen, I need all this stuff done. You should have been able to do it all today, but you're slow . . . as usual. It has to go out in the morning. You need to stay and finish this." Even though she's now an adult, her father is still controlling her with his critical eye.

Dad, are you treating your daughter the way you'd want to be treated?

Signs You Are Too Critical

- Your kid draws a picture and tears it up before your eyes because it's not good enough.
- Your kid takes a test and says, "I really blew it." Later you found out she got an A.
- Your kid puts herself down before you can.

The perfectionistic, critical-eyed parent most likely grew up with criticism himself. That's why it's important to put your critical eye in a storage unit for the rest of your and your daughter's lives. It's not easy to keep criticism bottled up, because it's so ingrained. Your first instinct is always to see the flaw. It's like an emotional or psychological virus that travels to your daughter.

Stan has a son and a daughter. His son, Michael, was handsome, a track star, an A student, and beloved by everybody, and he had a personality that drew everyone to him. His daughter,

Cheryl, two years younger, was average in looks, was a B student, and didn't seem to excel at anything. Stan didn't realize until Cheryl married after college how much of an impact his criticism had on his daughter.

"My son-in-law is a carbon copy of me, but even more critical," Stan says. "I can see how my criticism beat my daughter down so that she didn't want to try anything, because she knew she couldn't do it as well as her brother. Now my son-in-law is doing the same thing to my daughter and my grandkids, and I'm seeing the impact in all of their lives. I'm working hard to change my responses in my interactions with my daughter and grandkids. But that's not enough. I wish someone would have sat me down and told me what I was doing to my daughter. I'm going to have that talk with my son-in-law. He may listen, he may not, but I'm at least going to try."

The Pros and Cons of Your Skills

How do you go about tweaking what you want to change?

First, tell yourself the truth about yourself. Admit that you are a flaw picker. There is no magic dust for this situation. One of the most resistant things to turn around is a personality. You've been perfectionistic and critical of yourself and others since you were a little kid. You were the kid who used to line up your trucks and LEGOs in military precision. You're most likely a firstborn or only-born child. The way you respond to life has been ingrained in you. If you want a relationship with your daughter, you're the one who has to change. Without change on your part first, you can't have a relationship with your daughter.

Second, realize your skills that help you get raises, bonuses, and rave reviews at work are the same skills that work against you in your personal life. Perfectionists are often engineers, math teachers, architects, accountants, English professors, or other similar occupations. In those professions, perfectionism has paid off. But it backfires when you use it with people you love. When you find the flaw in your daughter, you're going to pay for it by shutting her down.

Third, because your tendencies to flaw-pick are ingrained, you're going to have to practice doing this. Your initial reaction will always be to find the flaw, and you'll fail miserably unless you stop and ask yourself, "What does the old me do?" And then, "What is the new me going to do differently?"

> While keeping your mouth shut, look for something positive to say.

If you don't keep your mouth shut while you're asking yourself those two questions, you will automatically do what you used to you. So, while keeping your mouth shut, look for something positive to say. Yes, in the beginning it'll be hard—kind of like trying to bend a river. But with practice and intentional action, the flow of water can cut a different kind of channel. You can gain success with baby steps of progress.

But making progress in this area is critical for your daughter's well-being both now and in the future. Criticizing a daughter wreaks havoc in her life. It makes her think, *I'm not worth anything.* If she doesn't think she's worth anything, whom will she gravitate to in her life? People who will treat her as if she's not worth it. She'll become a dishrag pleaser, the kind of woman people walk all over and abuse, whether at work, in her marriage, or with her other relationships. Is that really what you want for your daughter?

Ask Dr. Leman

Q: I just read *The Birth Order Book* and realize I've been the epitome of a critical-eyed parent. It grieves me to know that the issues my ten-year-old daughter is dealing with are directly attributed to how I've parented her. I always knew the right way to do things, and that was *my way* of doing things. I thought I was doing the right thing by holding her accountable and being tough on her. Now I realize that's been a big mistake. Is it possible to turn things around? If so, how?

A: Yes, you can turn things around. But the first important thing you need to realize is that, right now, you don't have a relationship with your daughter. Your entire connection has been built on rules and doing things your way. She hasn't had any say in the matter. What you have to do first is apologize. That's the only and the best way to start a relationship.

"Honey, I've come to the conclusion that your dad has made a complete fool of himself. I didn't realize it until now. I've acted like there's only one way to get things done, and that's my way. I've been very wrong, and I need to ask for your forgiveness."

Then you need to come alongside your daughter, listen to her, encourage her, and go out of your way to hear her perspective. Old habits will die hard, so you'll have to work very hard to think before you speak or act. What did you used to do? What should you do now? What will you do differently? It would be to your daughter's and your benefit to read two of my books: *Have a New You by Friday* and *Why Your Best Is Good Enough*.

Why Changing Your Ways Is So Important for Your Daughter

Many have wondered how Hillary Rodham Clinton has withstood the public humiliation of her husband's infidelity. Well, here's a clue: Hillary's dad was a textbook World War II–style dad. He actually trained troops for combat in the 1940s, though he himself never saw combat or left the States. Eventually he became the owner and sole employee of his own business, making drapes. Hillary described him as "a self-sufficient, tough-minded, small businessman."[3]

However, he was not an affirming father. On one telling occasion, Hillary brought home a report card with straight As. "My father's only comment," Hillary remembers, "was, 'Well, Hillary, that must be an easy school you go to.'" Another time he said, "Well, Hillary, how are you going to dig yourself out of this one?"[4]

In her book *It Takes a Village,* Hillary notes, "Children without fathers, or whose parents float in and out of their lives after divorce, are precarious little boats in the most turbulent seas."[5]

What she doesn't say—but what she has unwittingly demonstrated—is that children who have critical-eyed fathers grow accustomed to the treatment they've received as children and expect to be treated that way when they grow up. The message in the Rodham home? Toughen up. Emotions show weakness of character. "Maybe that's why she's such an accepting person," Hillary's mother, Dorothy, has said of her daughter. "She had to put up with him."[6]

As a practicing psychologist, I've found few generalizations to be all that accurate, but there's one in particular that, unfortunately, holds pretty true: most women who grow up with perfectionistic, critical fathers have high expectations of themselves. Though they may seem successful on the outside, they often feel like failures on the inside.

They also tend to marry exactly the wrong man. I've seen many women who have been scarred by their fathers then stack the deck against themselves to prove they're not worth anything—like their fathers told them.

Jenna's first husband—a handsome guy she'd quickly fallen in love with in high school—was abusive and controlling. When they divorced, he moved and refused to pay childcare, leaving her and their two young children nearly destitute. Jenna worked three jobs to provide for herself and the kids. When she met Frank, an older guy, she was certain he was "the one." He wanted to be involved in her and the kids' lives—something her father and ex-husband never were. But when they married, it didn't take long before she saw Frank for who he truly was: a womanizer, an alcoholic, and someone who sponged off others and had barely worked a day in his life.

> Most women who grow up with perfectionistic, critical fathers have high expectations of themselves.

Why does Jenna migrate toward losers? Because doing so reinforces the image she has of herself from her critical dad—that she's not worth loving.

Sadly, to make things even worse, women who have a low view of women invariably find men with a low view of women. Ironically, it takes a strong father to give a woman a high view of femininity. Daughters who are loved and affirmed by their fathers consider themselves worth being loved, so they pursue men who treat them like Daddy does.

Dad, that's why it's critical you pay attention to your daughter now—that you love her unconditionally and affirm her. If you don't, she may pay for that lack of attention the rest of her life with a disastrous marital choice. It will also greatly affect the way she and her husband treat your grandkids.

If you're a woman, and you're reading this chapter, it's crucial that you also understand the role the critical eye plays in relationships. A woman's relationship with her father will indelibly stamp the way she treats her sons. Remember what I said about how it's the cross-gender relationships that pack the most punch? Men need to be aware of this dynamic to help bring balance; women need to be aware of it to help right a family ship that is listing.

The time to do both is right now.

Daddy Tune-Up

Ask yourself:

- Am I quick to react?
- Do I prejudge people and situations?
- Do I jump to conclusions?
- Is my automatic answer no?
- Do I have a short fuse?
- Am I great at finding the flaw? A nitpicker?
- Do I have the need to be right?
- Do I blame others for my own shortcomings?

If you replied yes to any of the above questions, you've got a critical eye.

"I Love You Just the Way You Are"

Andrea, an only child, was a high school sophomore—beautiful, smart, and well liked by teachers and peers. In fact, all pointed to her as an example of a teenager who would achieve great heights someday. She got almost all As on her report card, was the track champion at her school, and started a group that volunteered after school at a shelter for abused animals.

Andrea was also three months pregnant. I met the family when her mother called me for help.

"Her father isn't taking this very well," she said with a tremor in her voice.

The first time I met with the family, the father refused to come. He said it wasn't his problem; it was Andrea's.

I'm a psychologist. I don't take that kind of guff. So I phoned him and insisted he come . . . now.

A very angry father stalked into the room a short while later. "She's the one who needs straightening out! And that boyfriend of hers! So why do you need to talk to me?"

Andrea had been dating the same boy for over a year. Nick was two years older and a senior. Both were good kids and top achievers. They had met while caring for an abused puppy at the shelter. Both had a heart, literally, for the underdog. The more I found out about them, I understood why. Andrea couldn't remember a time when her father had said he loved her; Nick couldn't remember his mother ever saying she loved him. Both teenagers had sensitive personalities that suffered greatly from parental criticism. That only drew the two closer for mutual comfort, and one night hormones took over.

"When I looked into Nick's eyes, and he said he loved me, I

realized, *Wow, this is the first time a guy has ever said that to me,*" Andrea told me.

"When was the last time your daddy said he loved you?" I asked.

She hung her head. "Never."

"Never?" I said.

Finally she whispered, "I was never good enough." She looked up at me, with tears in her eyes. "I wish he'd said it even once."

Now that's a tragedy. At that moment, I wanted to punch that dad right where it counts for what he'd done to his daughter.

> When was the last time you told your daughter, "I love you"?

Dad, when was the last time you told your daughter, "I love you"? Or do you simply assume she knows it? Do you treat her like the precious treasure she is, or does she constantly have to jump over the high bar of your expectations?

It's time to bring the classic Billy Joel lyric into play: "I love you just the way you are."

Go ahead—practice the words if you can't say them right away. If you tend to have that critical eye, go out of your way to affirm and encourage because your imprinted tendency will be to nitpick.

One of the most fundamental needs for a human being is acceptance. Your daughter is going to belong someplace. So where will that be? With you, or in someone else's arms?

If you were to ask each of my kids, "Who's Daddy's favorite?" I bet each would whisper, "Don't tell the others, but I'm sure that it's me." They all think they're the favorite—and I work to preserve each one's treasured place in my heart. In fact, all have nicknames I've given them. For example, Hannah is "Daddy's little peanut." Lauren is "Daddy's little muffin." One time I got tired and referred to Lauren as "Daddy's little peanut" and was rebuked with a vigorous, "I'm not Daddy's little peanut; I'm Daddy's little muffin!" That's another thing I learned as a father of daughters. You don't mix up your daughters' nicknames—ever.

Your daughter needs your affirmation; she longs to belong to you, to hold that treasured place in your heart.

What happened to Andrea, Nick, and their baby? They were unusually mature teenagers. Knowing they weren't ready for marriage or parenting, they decided to grant another couple the gift of adoption. With the help of their wise school administrator, Andrea was able to move into an older couple's home nearby and finish her last few months of sophomore year through home-study. Nick brought her homework each night and went to doctor visits with her. Their baby was born in the summer, with Nick in the delivery room. As Nick held their baby, the first thing he whispered was, "Oh, here you are, finally. Like a little angel. I love you, my girl."

Andrea started sobbing. They were the words she'd longed to hear from her father for so long. Now they were the first words her little girl heard from her father.

Today Andrea is a sophomore in college. Nick is a senior at the same college. They're no longer dating each other, but neither is dating anyone else. They're focusing on growing their friendship, realizing it will be the best way to form a solid foundation for marriage, should they choose to go that way in the future. Both are still achievers—Andrea aiming to become a veterinarian and Nick a high school teacher. Two Saturdays a month they volunteer at a local animal shelter. One weekend a month they drive to visit their now four-year-old daughter at her adopted parents' home. They never leave without each of them telling little Nicole, "I love you."

Such simple words.

But they make a mountain of difference to your daughter—both now and in her future.

A Good Dad's Quick Reference Guide

- Affirm instead of flaw-pick.
- Say "I love you" always and often.

EIGHT

A Cake Without Sugar

Why buying your daughter stuff and popping in and out of her life will never satisfy what she wants most—you.

It was Sande's and my anniversary, and my daughter was determined to bake us a cake. She didn't want any help. She could do it herself, thank you very much.

The resulting cake was awful, to tell you the truth. But I knew the day would come when this daughter of mine would be able to make chocolate chip cookies and cakes that actually tasted good, so I didn't want to discourage her on her first try.

Of course, it didn't help that she had broiled the cake instead of baked it. "I just turned the oven on," she explained. "How was I supposed to know the other dial was set to broil?"

Fair enough. After she scraped off the top crust, the "cake" was about an inch high. She piled it with frosting to remind us that it wasn't brownies, then served a piece to my wife and me.

"This is so . . . moist," Sande said delicately. "I can't believe how moist this is."

"Delicious, honey," I added, choking a bite down. "Could I

139

get another cup of milk? . . . While you are at it, why don't you bring the entire carton?" Our daughter's smile was worth the deception.

The next morning Sande was rummaging through the cupboards. "Where's the powdered milk? I bought a whole box a few days ago, and now I can't find it."

"Powdered milk?" my daughter asked.

Sande swiveled in time to see our daughter's eyes dart to the infamous "cake."

"You mean that wasn't flour?" my daughter asked.

Sande burst out laughing, and our daughter joined her. No wonder the cake seemed so moist!

Cakes are relatively easy to make, but if you change even one essential ingredient, like flour, or you leave out the sugar, the result will be a disaster. The fundamental ingredient in any woman's life is her relationship with her father. If that is missing or distorted, she will have to spend a good bit of time and energy overcoming the deficit. If a daughter hasn't experienced unconditional love and acceptance with her daddy, she may tell herself she's loved when a guy shows interest in her, when all she really has is a sexual relationship. It's cake but without the sugar that makes a lifelong connection so sweet.

Some of you fathers and daughters haven't had an easy road with each other, but that doesn't mean things can't improve. This chapter will start you in the right direction.

The "Stuff-y" Dad

Marcia, a single mom of two daughters, told me, "I divorced a year ago. My ex lives in Florida and has a really good job, while the girls and I struggle on my more limited income. He flies in one day, spends seven hundred bucks on our daughters, and then leaves the next day. I'm left to mop up the mess."

Marcia noticed that it always took a few days to get back to normal in her house. Her girls were mouthy and critical, and their talk focused on what they didn't have and wanted rather than on what they did have. Getting stuff from their dad only increased their desire for more stuff. They were becoming the Disneyland and Toys-R-Us kids, and Marcia hated that.

But Marcia also told me, "It was interesting that the girls always talked about what they did together—where they went and what he bought them. They never really talked about their dad and didn't seem to relate to him much. He was merely the tag-along person who financed everything."

It's tempting to want to buy your daughters things, isn't it? It's hard not to want to lavish on your daughters all the things you couldn't have as a kid. But don't do it. Don't make your relationship about things instead of the two of you. Things don't last. Whether you're living at home with your daughter or living elsewhere, what your daughter wants more than anything is you—your time, your presence.

> Don't make your relationship about things instead of the two of you.

Steve dotes on his only child, a daughter. His family is a middle-class one, but he loves to provide Jana with surprises. For her eighth birthday, he paid for all the girls in her school class to go with her to Build-a-Bear. For her twelfth birthday, he sent Jana and three of her friends on a plane ride to stay with her aunt on Martha's Vineyard for a week. For her thirteenth birthday, he bought her a chocolate diamond ring. Then he started saving up to buy her a red Corvette for her sixteenth birthday. But look carefully at each of those experiences. Steve paid for them, but where was he? MIA at the event. He provided the experiences, but he wasn't there. Why not? Because he was working the extra hours to pay for them.

His wife, Janet, the commonsense one in the family, told me, "By providing everything Jana wants, and more, he's turning her into a brat. There, I said it. My daughter is a brat. I don't even like to be around her anymore. When I told her no about getting something last week, she glared at me and said, 'I'll ask Dad. He'll get it for me,' and flounced out the door. I wanted to wring her neck . . . but I want to wring his more."

After Janet and I talked, she decided to have a heart-to-heart with that hubby of hers. He was at first very defensive about his desire to provide for the family. But she pushed ahead. She was determined that things change in their family. "Providing the basics is one thing," she insisted. "Turning her into the 'I gotta have everything' kid is another." Then she threw in what I told her about "Stuff-y" dads and asked him, "Steve, are you giving her all these things to make sure that Jana likes you?"

That hit home. Steve hung his head. He realized he was. And he also realized he was patterning his parenting after his dad's. Steve could remember only one time when his dad had spent time with him—when his dad arranged for an expensive two-week fishing trip. Otherwise, his dad was emotionally and physically unavailable.

"What made that fishing trip so special?" she asked Steve.

Then he began pouring out his feelings and his desires to feel his dad's love. But he said he'd always felt disconnected from his dad, who provided many things for him but never engaged with him. Yet all Steve wanted was to feel loved, affirmed, understood, and as though he belonged to his daddy.

"Do you think that's what Jana might want more than any-thing, too," Janet said, "but maybe she doesn't know how to voice it? Could all these things you give her be replacing what she really needs—you?"

Steve got it. He and his wife are now unified in their desire to make their family about relating to each other, not about things. The road won't be easy, as Jana is nearing fourteen. She had her first wake-up call when she presented an extravagant plan last week for her upcoming fourteenth birthday with friends and Steve said no . . . and stuck with no.

Jana posted on Facebook later that day: *My parental units have gone crazy.*

And she hasn't seen anything yet. However, if Steve and Janet stick with the plan they came up with, they can turn their "Stuff-y" dad situation around and start to groom a grateful daughter instead of a "gimme" daughter.

A Wake-Up Call

I grew up in a blue-collar home that barely covered the basics. Extras weren't even in the "wishing" category. When I got married and started a family, I didn't want them to lack for any-thing, the way I did as a kid. After my daughter was born, I started working a longer shift at the factory. Long story short, my daughter is now seven, and I don't often see her because she's in bed when I get home. One day last month I arrived at the factory to find out it was closed for the day due to electrical wiring issues. While I was driving home, I heard you talk about

"Stuff-y" dads on the radio. What you said smacked me right between the eyes. My daughter only had a half day of school that day, so I shocked her and my wife by saying, "What would you guys like to do today?" What they wanted was so simple. We packed up peanut butter and jelly sandwiches, pickles, chips, Oreos, a picnic blanket, and a Frisbee, and drove to a local park. We spent the entire afternoon playing together and laughing together. Then we sat on the blanket and watched the sun set as we finished off the chips and Oreos.

When we were getting back in the car, my daughter threw her arms around me. "Dad, this has been the best day of my life, because I've spent it with you."

My wife nodded, all teary-eyed.

Wow. I hate thinking what I've missed for seven years. My wife and I talked long into the night about what really mattered. The next morning, I notified my boss that I wanted to transition out of taking the longer shift and switch to the regular shift. "I have a daughter at home who needs me," was the only explanation I gave him.

In less than a month, I'll be on the regular shift rotation. We may be eating a lot more PB&J from now on, and our "vacations" may be at that park instead of a plane ride away, but now my wife, my daughter, and I are a team. Where one goes, we all go. And I love it that way.

—Roger, Illinois

What You Don't Give Your Daughter . . . and What You Do

Some of you reading this book are on tight incomes. Rather than stew over what you lack and can't give your kids, focus on what you *can* give them. When I come home from a business trip, you won't find my suitcase filled with presents for my kids. I didn't want the focus of my return to be on trinkets, but on the joy of renewing our relationship in person. So why would I want to give them a toy that they'd immediately want to run off and play with when, more than anything, I want time with them?

So does that mean I *never* bring them home anything? No, occasionally I'll come across something on the road that fits one of my children well, and I'll buy it. Like the time I bought Krissy a cute little lamp at a minimall. She'd needed one for quite some time, and it was just her style. But that present was based on a relationship, and not on guilt or obligation. My rule is that if I get one child a gift, I don't feel like I have to get each child a gift. If I did, with rearing five kids in the house and as much traveling as I do for a living, I'd be bankrupt. Life isn't always "fair and square," and the sooner your kids learn that, the better.

For example, fast-forward to Holly's response when I brought home the lamp for Krissy and nothing for her: "But that's not fair!"

"Do you really want me to treat you the way I treat your little sister?"

"Yes." She sniffled.

"Okay, your bedtime is now 8:30 instead of 9:00. Oh, and your allowance is now two dollars instead of three dollars."

> "But that's not fair!"

The sniffles stopped. "What?"

"You said you wanted to be treated the same."

"Uh, I didn't mean that."

I wanted Holly to understand that from time to time I might find something that was perfect for one of my daughters, but that didn't obligate me to try to come up with a meaningless gift for everyone else, all in the name of "fairness." Each daughter deserves her day in the sun and should be favored from time to time. That's what makes her feel special.

I tried to keep that in mind as my girls grew, even in the small decisions I made.

Every Saturday, Holly and I read the newspaper together and talked over the news. We fell into a routine—I immediately handed her the "Life" and "Dear Abby" sections, and she knew I got to read the sports section first. This tradition became part of our special relationship.

On Fridays, I always brought the kids a treat from the bakery. It would have been easiest to tell the baker, "Give me a half dozen maple doughnuts," but that wouldn't have been nearly as meaningful to my children. Instead, I picked out what I knew they liked best.

Holly and Kevin always wanted chocolate éclairs. So did Hannah, most of the time, but every so often she liked to mix it up with a doughnut. Lauren had to have a doughnut with sprinkles. She'd lick off the sprinkles and frosting and throw away the rest. Krissy liked dainty little cakes called petits fours.

Every Friday, with this simple act of choosing treats from the bakery, I reinforced the following message to my children: "There are five of you, but I know each one of you very well. I don't take you for granted. I never forget that you are individuals. You matter to me." Do you think my daughters got the message? Take a peek at pages 229–30 if you wonder. Keep in mind that my daughters now span the ages of twenty-one through forty-two.

Making each daughter feel special and uniquely loved is one of the best gifts a father can give his daughter.

What Your Daughter Is Waiting For—From You

Being a good dad isn't about playing Santa Claus; it's about building a daddy-daughter connection. Dad, when you buy your daughter things to replace your relationship, you might think you're keeping her close, in your court, but the opposite is true. Throwing her a bone—a gift—might make you feel like you've done something, but all you've done is push her away from you. When I asked twelve-year-old Morie about her dad, she shrugged. "I don't see him much. But he takes me out somewhere cool on my birthday, we do something big for spring break, and then maybe do a couple big vacations in the summer." Here's the kicker: that dad comes home to his wife and daughter every night . . . but then does his own thing. He lives at home and provides for his family through his job, but he doesn't connect at heart with them.

Think of it this way. Every day your daughter is asking you this question, whether she voices it out loud or not: "How important am I to you, really?"

Like the time Krissy and I were having breakfast together and a man walked up to me and asked me to be a speaker for a men's retreat on May 16. The instant the date came out of the man's mouth, Krissy kicked me forcefully under the table. I didn't want to be impolite and cut the guy off, so I let him keep talking . . . and received another sharp kick from Krissy.

> Being a good dad isn't about playing Santa Claus; it's about building a daddy-daughter connection.

Finally, with a glare and another sharp kick looming in my near future, I said to the man, "It's very kind of you to think of me, but I have an important engagement on May 16. That day just happens to be my daughter's birthday."

There was an audible sigh across the table. Krissy was waiting for me to voice the words that proved to her she was a priority in my life.

Dad, if your daughter doesn't feel important in your life, that affirmation may come with a big price tag—sexually transmitted diseases, unwed pregnancy, and a host of other consequences. If your daughter is starved for your affection, she'll be putty in the hands of those who want to use and abuse her.

What is your daughter waiting for from you? If you asked her, what would make her feel most prized right now? Bet you anything that spending time with you is at the heart of that request.

Cydnee wanted to go fishing.

Amanda wanted to explore a cave.

Joy wanted to lie on the roof of their house and look at the stars.

But what was the common thread in all of these requests of the girls?

They wanted to do those things with dear ol' Dad.

The In-N-Out Dad

I love In-N-Out burgers. My growing physique is partly a result of them. There's nothing tastier than one of those burgers and a heap of fries. Every once in a while I feel guilty and try something like the "no carb" diet. But then I'm on the road, and those burgers tantalize me again.

In-N-Out burgers are fabulous. But In-N-Out dads? They're downright toxic to a daughter.

A divorced dad once told me, "I gotta go see my kid next weekend and take her on this Girl Scout canoe trip since it's not my ex's thing."

Note the wording the dad used: "I gotta go." Not, "I can't wait to spend a weekend with my daughter. We're going on a Girl Scout canoe trip together." He approached his relationship with his daughter as a "have to," not a "want to." Do you think his daughter has noticed that attitude? Frankly, how could she miss it?

There are many names for the kind of dads who drop in and out of their daughters' lives: "hit and run" dads; "drop gifts off and leave" dads, "so many things to do" dads, "got another family" dads. But it all comes down to the same thing—they're dads who pop in and out of their daughters' lives when they feel like it. After all, life's busy; they've got a business to run and their social lives to maintain, you know?

These dads can be single or married again, living in the same town or far away. The point is that they could make their daughters a priority, but they've chosen to relate to those daughters only when it's convenient for them. Their daughters become afterthoughts, something to fit into the schedule if there's time. And if that dad has a second family, there's rarely time, not to mention he'll catch an earful from his current wife if he spends time hanging around his first family very long.

> Their daughters become afterthoughts, something to fit in the schedule if there's time.

Even more toxic is the dad who shows up every third year, because he's "supposed to" see his daughter, spends some money on her (probably out of guilt), and then leaves. In between, all that dad is to the daughter is an envelope that comes in the mail to her mother, with the court-mandated support payments. These are the ones I call the losers, the deadbeats, and the abuser dads. But my best guess is that none of you dads reading this book are in that category, since losers, deadbeats, and abusive dads wouldn't care enough about their relationships with their daughters to take the time to read a book titled *Be the Dad She Needs You to Be.* If you're a daughter or a mom reading this book, the sooner you "lose" that dad, the better off you'll be. In my counseling cases, the mothers and daughters are much better off without such a toxic male influence.

There's no way a daughter can feel close to that kind of dad, nor should she unless he decides he wants to change completely and become an involved dad. Many girls in that situation end up creating a sort of fantasy father, the close kind of dad they long for: a dad who supports them emotionally, who takes a genuine interest in what they're interested in.

In-N-Out dads are toxic material to a girl who is learning how to relate to males. Such a dad's lack of interest tells her that she's not valuable, that she's not worth spending time with, and that no males are trustworthy. Those messages will lead her to all sorts of poor relational choices with those of the male gender.

Dad, your attention is what she craves most of all. If you say you love your daughter, why would you not want to spend time with her and be involved in her life? If popping in and out of your daughter's life has been your pattern, how can you change it?

No matter what age your daughter is—from babyhood to teenager—she needs you. She needs to bond with you. She needs to know that you're a safe place to land and that you'll always be there for her. And if she doesn't see you all the time on a regular basis, she isn't going to bond with you. Young kids, in particular, have very sharp memories.

Take a Careful Look at Your Schedule

Record your daughter's events as your first priorities outside your regular workday, not your last priority, when it can fit in. When she has an event, show up if you're local. If you're long-distance, call her or text her right before the event; then do the same thing after the event.

Research Activities Your Daughter Is Interested In

Take your focus off giving her gifts, and substitute activities you can do together. If this one thing doesn't change, nothing in your relationship will change. You have to spend time together to reestablish your connection. Find ways in which you can participate with her in those activities she enjoys. If she likes rock-climbing, find a local rock-climbing wall and try it out with her. If she likes concerts, take her to one, even if it's not the sort of music you like. If she likes to paint ceramics, it won't kill you to sit beside her and paint a dog or cat at the mall. Bet she'd love to have the one you painted with her, too, and she would display it proudly in her bedroom. Even more important, it's a reminder of the fact, *Daddy loves me.*

Show Her You Think of Her Throughout the Day

Send little texts. Create inside jokes between the two of you. Find fun videos and pictures to make her laugh and send her the links.

Make Regular Appointments

If you live in the same town, go out of your way to make at least one night a week "Dad and Daughter" night. If you live a distance apart, make frequent trips to see your daughter, and use Skype or FaceTime so you can talk regularly, face to face.

Ask Her Opinion on Issues You Face

Your daughter needs to know you value her opinion. If you make that clear to her, she'll also be more likely to share her own questions or issues she's facing with you. But there's a huge difference between asking a question and asking for an opinion. Kids don't like questions. Their defenses go up immediately. But saying, "You're really good at problem solving, and I'd like your advice on something," shows that you value what your daughter thinks. She will welcome that kind of interaction and will go away from it feeling confident about her needed role in your family.

Do What You Promise

Felicia remembers clearly when her dad told her he and his mom were getting divorced. She was five years old. He promised that even though he wouldn't be living with them anymore, he'd call her three times a week and come get her to stay with him on the weekend. That promise lasted for one week—the first week he was out of the house. He never did come to get her on the weekend.

Sondra remembers when her dad always promised to take her shopping "tomorrow," but tomorrow never came. He was too drunk to remember most of the time, and when he did remember, he evidently decided other things were more important than his daughter.

If you were those girls, how would you feel? Angry? Betrayed? Ticked off at the male population in general? Who can blame them? The primary person in their lives, the one they thought they could trust, lied to them and let them down. Is it any wonder these girls develop into women with trust issues and they usually carry a lot of anger toward males in general? They also feel insecure in their relationships with men since they believed what their daddy said—until he didn't follow through with those promises. Many spend years stuffing their feelings of loss, betrayal, and abandonment down deep. They don't know why they keep pursuing men who are bad for them. They can't separate love from lust. They offer excuses for the men who hurt them and blame themselves. What's the little girl in them really saying? *If I would have been a better person, or done this or that, my daddy would have loved me and wanted to spend time with me. He would never have left me or my mother.*

Imperfect dads produce imperfect daughters who pay for their fathers' mistakes with more mistakes of their own.

Dads who are trustworthy, never lie, can be counted on, and follow through on their promises produce trusting, healthy, balanced daughters who find trustworthy men who don't lie, can be counted on, and follow through on their promises. If there is pain and brokenness in your family from divorce, separation, or disillusionment, the time to change the pattern is now, before it affects the next generation of your family.

The first step is deciding to change yourself.

The second step is changing yourself.

You can do it, if you choose to do it.

If You Want Your Daughter to Trust You . . .

. . . become someone your daughter can trust.

Especially for Divorced Dads

If you've divorced and left home, assuaging your guilt by taking your daughter to Disneyland or turning into the "Gift Daddy" does nothing to build her trust or your daddy-daughter connection. Regardless of the spin you put on it, you've already betrayed her trust by divorcing her mother and deciding you wanted a life elsewhere, away from your family. Or perhaps your wife divorced you. Now, to get back at your ex and to buy your daughter's love, you're providing days packed with excitement and spending a wad when your kids are with you. How can your ex compete with that? Typically, most women make less than men, even if they're working full-time. It's a recipe for relational disaster, with the smart daughter learning how to play Mom and Dad against each other to get what she wants.

I'll be frank. You and your ex divorced for a reason—and that included not being able to get along. But divorcing each other doesn't mean you're no longer mom and dad to your daughter. For that daughter's sake, lay down your weapons for a few minutes and talk through what's best for her. Come up with a game plan that works for all of you. That includes basic rules that are a part of everyday life, such as bedtime, eating, and dating habits, so that your daughter doesn't get tossed back and forth between two very different universes each time she switches houses, if that's what the divorce decree stipulates. Then agree that neither of you will grill your daughter about what she does when she's at the "other house." Since women are relational, your ex will always want to ask your daughter upon her return from your house, "How late were you out? What did you eat? You look really tired—are you sure you're okay?" These grilling sessions will plant seeds of doubt and mistrust in your daughter about how you are treating her. But if you adhere to this agreement, you and your

> Agree that neither of you will grill your daughter about what she does when she's at the "other house."

daughter both will be secure in your love and safe care of her when she's with you.

There are two things you must do for your daughter:

1. *Be there for her physically and emotionally.* No matter what it takes, make her well-being a priority. If you haven't done this in this past, if you've focused on your own welfare instead, you'll need to win her trust once again. That means you make plans to spend time with her and support her in little ways, and then you follow through on what you say you'll do.

2. *Go the extra mile to support your ex.* Your ex may be your ex, but a long time ago, you made her and your daughter your family. Real men take care of their families, even if the situation is far from ideal. Yes, your ex could be a real piece of work, but she is still your daughter's mother. Don't ever bad-mouth your ex. In fact, you should be doing everything you can to help her. Put in writing that you'll continue to pay for your daughter's private education and that you'll continue your spousal support at least through your daughter's high school graduation so that your ex can focus on what she needs to do most in these remaining years with your daughter at home—be there with your daughter. Start putting aside money to help your daughter with college, if she is so inclined.

Too many men leave their families and start new lives, perhaps with new families, leaving their first families in the dust as if they never existed. If you've done that with your daughter, it's time to make amends. Not only do you need to ask her and your ex for forgiveness, you need to clarify what you will do differently and then do it differently from that point on. If you drop the ball, you won't be able to reestablish a relationship of trust with your daughter.

How to Talk with Your Girl

- Don't give ready answers . . . or even have all the answers.
- Don't "should" on her. (You "should" do this or that.)
- Strive for a soft landing and your words will have more impact.
- Try, "Sounds interesting. Tell me more about that."
- Do what you say you'll do.

Some of you are rolling your eyes right now. *There is no way my ex is going to accept an apology from me . . . not now, not ever.* But to reestablish your daddy-daughter connection, you still need to do your part with both mama and daughter. Your part is to apologize genuinely for what you did wrong and ask for forgiveness. Whether the other party extends that forgiveness is up to her. You can't control others' reactions; you can only control your responses. For your relationship with your daughter to change, you need to make right all that is in your power to make right.

Is it possible for things to change? Yes! Jason and his daughter Kyra, now fourteen, are living proof. Jason had an affair, divorced his wife, and left to start a new life with his girlfriend, who was pregnant. Six months later, he married Megan, and their baby was born.

Kyra was nine when her half sister was born. "All I can remember is Mom crying every night after my daddy disappeared," she says. "I never really understood what happened until a lot later."

Jason disappeared for nearly four years from Kyra's life, and Kyra grew angry. "I told people I hated my dad. But all I really wanted, deep inside, was for him to be in my life and hug me again."

Then, a year ago, Jason had an experience that can only be described as a "complete change." He met God Almighty in a personal way. Over the past year, he has asked Kyra and her mother for forgiveness, paid for a new roof on their house, and invited both over to his home for a picnic. "The first time I went there was really weird," Kyra admits, "and I could tell my mom didn't want to go.

> Jason disappeared for nearly four years from Kyra's life.

But she did it for me, and because Dad came over and told her how sorry he was for wronging her the way he did. I think she was so shocked she didn't even yell. She said yes to going to his house."

When Kyra met her almost four-year-old sister, she fell in love with Natalie's toothy smile. Jason's second wife, Megan, had met God within a few months of when Jason did, and she warmly welcomed Kyra and her mom. Now Kyra spends weekends with her father, sister, and Megan, and the weekdays with her mom. Megan surprised Kyra by suggesting they turn their den into a bedroom for her. Together the two picked out the paint and decorations and worked on the room each weekend. "That gave me a chance to get to know Megan as a person, instead of only as the wicked you-know-what who had stolen my dad from my mom and me. She, too, told me she was sorry for what had happened, and then told me how both she and Dad had changed and wanted to do things differently from now on."

Kyra's mom has declined going over to her ex's house more than the one time. "But I can tell she's relieved that I have my dad back in my life now, and she doesn't feel so alone when she needs help with bigger things, like replacing the roof," Kyra says. "Dad even showed up when I told him our toilet was leaking and fixed it while Mom was at work."

That family has experienced a miracle. Yes, with God anything is possible. But it also took a human being's determination. Jason had to own up to what he did and ask for forgiveness. Without that major first step, Kyra's daddy wouldn't be back in her life right now.

What would it take for you to reestablish a positive daddy-daughter connection? Why not take the first step toward it today?

For Daughters Only

If you read the title of this book, *Be the Dad She Needs You to Be,* and you said, "Well, I wish my dad were like that," you're not alone.

As Jessica said, "I never see my birth dad. He exited our lives when I was eleven. Now the stepdad I've lived with for four years is the guy who picks me up from cheerleading."

"I wish my dad were my 'best man,' like you talk about," Donna shared. "Instead, he was around the house, like a piece of furniture, but never really available."

"I lived in fear of my dad," Marian admitted. "He was a church elder on Sundays, and the rest of the week he beat my mom and sometimes me. But still he'd make us go to church with him and act all righteous. One time when she had a black eye, he made her stay home and told me I had to tell people she had the flu. He threatened to beat me if I told anybody the truth. So I find it hard to even relate to a 'caring daddy.' There was no such thing in my world."

"My mom ran our house," Wendi said. "My dad was a real

wimp. He brought in money through his computer business but did nothing else. I always wanted him to be the kind of guy I could count on to get in our neighborhood bully's face when he tripped me on the way home from school, but I knew I had to handle it myself. My dad wasn't somebody I could count on to be my protector."

Some of you grew up with not only emotionally or physically distant dads but abusive dads. You suffered the marks of physical abuse, and the verbal and psychological slams from your father still haunt you to this day.

If you're an abuse survivor, you may find yourself thinking, *I'm not good enough. I'll never be good enough.* Such thought patterns became your life mantra because the one person you needed to love you, support you, and protect you—your daddy—didn't provide those basic needs in your life. Some of you, as a result, have fulfilled your own *I'm not good enough* prophecy by dating or marrying men who are as abusive to you as your father was to you and your mother.

But I want to be clear. You were not put on this earth to be anyone's whipping post, whether in words or lashes. You need to get away from any abusive men in your life immediately. Don't take the "wait and see" approach. Run!

Extending Grace and Forgiveness

I know a woman who's in her forties. Her dad is in his seventies. Stephanie and her dad have always had a rocky relationship for as long as she can remember. When her dad celebrated his seventy-fifth birthday, something happened. He grew softer, not as bull-headed, though he's still a hard case to be around. But the biggest change is in his daughter.

When Stephanie hit the big 4-0, she did some soul-searching and realized she'd struggled a lot in life because of her dad's negative imprinting. She thought back to her childhood, when she put her dad on a pedestal—at least for a while. But because he wasn't by nature the warm, comforting presence she saw in her best friend's father, Stephanie never felt loved. As she headed into her adult years, she closed herself off from her dad. For years, they'd only related politely about surface subjects, never digging deeply. On her birthday, it struck her that her dad had tried to love her in the only way he knew how—by making sure the mortgage payment was paid and that she had a warm coat and boots without holes in winter. His love language was being a good provider. Did he provide the emotional support she needed? Far from it. But he'd tried, more than she ever realized, in his own way.

In that moment, she decided to approach her father differently. With hard work, determination, and a lot of effort, she started to get to know her father again. When she cut him some slack for being human, she saw glimpses of things she appreciated and connected them to positive childhood memories. They now have a far different relationship than they did only a few years ago. Is it perfect? No. But both are working on it.

With imperfect dads, you can either major in the minors and drive yourself crazy, or you can accept your dad for the very imperfect person he is and go on. A dad who doesn't love his daughter wouldn't go into a coal mine or a factory every day. He had a reason for doing that . . . and the reason was you and your mom.

If you had an abusive dad, you need to forgive him, even if you are not able to meet him in a safe location to extend that forgiveness to him. How he responds to your overture isn't something you can control. Saying, "I forgive you"—whether in person, in a letter or e-mail, or on the phone—frees *you* from the confines of your past relationship that will otherwise continue to control your life, your thoughts, and your relationships. When you do that, you'll feel the release of years' worth of hurts. You deserve to soar in your relationships. Don't allow the past to weigh you down in such a way.

Does forgiveness mean that you reconnect as dad and daughter in situations of abuse? It's not as likely, and in many situations, it wouldn't be safe or healthy for you to do so, especially if the patterns of abuse remain in your father and his life has not done a 180. Never, ever allow yourself to become his physical or psychological punching bag for any reason.

It's All About the Relationship

I talked with a dad last week who was struggling with his teenage daughter.

"She knows that our rule is no dating until you're sixteen, and she's only fourteen," he told me. "But I discovered she's been sneaking around, seeing this guy she met on the Internet. I've taken away everything I thought would mean something to her— her iPhone, her iPod, and her computer—to nip the relationship in the bud, but nothing works. She acts like it doesn't matter. What can I do?"

"First of all," I said, "nothing you take away from her will mean jack. Those are only things. What you're missing is a relationship. As my friend Josh McDowell says, 'Rules without relationship lead to rebellion.' Your daughter won't care what you think until she has a relationship with you. That's where you need to start."

Dad, do you really have a heart connection with your daughter? Or is your relationship defined by you giving her stuff or popping in and out of her life at your convenience or when work isn't too busy?

How can you start toward a relationship? By first owning your role in the disconnect. You start by approaching her and saying the two hardest words in the English language for us men to say: "I'm sorry." We tough guys are afraid that doing so will show our weakness. Actually, it does the opposite. It shows our strength. Only weak people are afraid of being wrong. Strong people learn through failure and making mistakes. To reestablish your relationship—the kind of connection you dreamed of when you held your little daughter in your arms for the first time—you need to show your willingness to enter your daughter's world and to show compassion (another difficult thing for us men).

You may live in a different home than your daughter, but you can still establish that heart connection if you choose to work at it. And it is just that—a choice. Again, your daughter won't care until you do. There are such things as e-mail, texting, Skype, phone calls, packages, letters, and visits. And believe me when I tell you that, to a female, a heartfelt handwritten note on a sweet card accomplishes a lot more in your connection than a Skype or FaceTime call.

Your daughter won't care until you do.

If your pattern has been to be the "Stuff-y" dad—giving her stuff when you feel guilty or to replace what's missing in your relationship—stop sending and giving presents. Those gifts will only alienate your daughter more and get her used to getting only stuff. Instead, work on your relationship. Text her little notes. Go out of your way to spend time together, whether that means a car ride or a plane ride. Focus on doing things together that she enjoys. Laugh together. Recall memories of easier early days.

If your pattern has been "the In-N-Out dad," you have a decision to make. Either you're in or you're out. Jerking your daughter back and forth between the two options does immeasurable harm to her relationship with any male in the future. If you're reading this book, then there's a good chance you want to be "in"; you probably just don't know how to do it. Getting involved in your daughter's life starts one step at a time. It means, though, putting her first. If you're divorced, that means she needs to be a top priority in your new life and your new relationships. If you truly want a relationship with her, you have to prove yourself— that you love her, that she's valuable to you, and that you are trustworthy and are going to be consistent in her life. All those things take time, steadiness, and patience, but you can do it. In fact, for your daughter's sake and for the sake of her future relationship with any of the male gender, you must do it.

Unfinished Business

For imperfect dads and daughters, life isn't easy. But humility, compassion, and forgiveness can turn your relationship around and get it headed in the right direction. And the time to do so is now. Years ago, I saw a story in *Guideposts* magazine that still tears me up, even though I've read it a dozen times since then.[1] Following is the condensed story, adapted by yours truly.

Sue, a registered nurse, was caring for a seriously ill man named Mr. Williams. He asked her to call his daughter.

"Of course," Sue said, but that wasn't good enough for Mr. Williams.

"Will you call her right away—as soon as you can?" he pleaded.

"I'll call her the very first thing," Sue assured him.

Right before she left the room, Mr. Williams asked Sue for a pencil and a piece of paper, and she gave both to him. Then she walked out to call the daughter.

As soon as she dialed the number she had been given and said "heart attack," she heard a loud scream on the other end of the line: "No! He's not dying, is he?"

"His condition is stable," Sue reported.

"You must not let him die," Janie, the daughter, begged. "My daddy and I haven't spoken in almost a year." She then explained that they had fought over a boyfriend. The argument ended with Janie running out of the house. Many times she had thought about calling her father and asking for forgiveness, but it never seemed to be the right time. "The last thing I said to him was, 'I hate you,'" she said through her sobs. "I'm coming. Now! I'll be there in thirty minutes."

> "You must not let him die," Janie, the daughter, begged. "My daddy and I haven't spoken in almost a year."

Sue hung up, then walked into Mr. Williams's room. He lay frighteningly still, and she couldn't find a pulse. He had suffered a cardiac arrest. Immediately she put out the alert: "Code 99. Room 712. Code 99. Stat!" and started performing CPR. As she did, she prayed, *God, his daughter is coming. Don't let it end this way.*

The emergency medical team rushed in with their equipment. A physician inserted a tube in Mr. Williams's mouth.

Nurses plunged syringes of medicine into the IV. Sue connected a heart monitor but was unable to detect a single beat.

The lead physician cried out, "Stand back," and took the paddles from Sue to shock Mr. Williams's heart back to life.

One hit. Two hits. Three hits.

Nothing.

Finally the doctors and nurses gave one another knowing looks. The lead physician shook his head. A nurse unplugged the oxygen.

Mr. Williams was dead.

When Sue left the room, she saw a young woman with wounded eyes slumped against the wall. A doctor had already delivered the information. Sue accompanied Janie into a quiet room.

"I never hated him," Janie sobbed. "I loved him."

She then asked to see her daddy, so Sue led her to Mr. Williams's bed. Janie buried her face in her dead father's sheets.

As Sue backed up, her hand fell on the scrap of paper she had handed to her patient moments before. A man's scrawl read:

My dearest Janie,

I forgive you. I pray you will also forgive me. I know that you love me. I love you too.

Daddy

The note shook in Sue's hands as she thrust it toward Janie. She read it once, then twice. Her tormented face grew radiant. Peace glistened in her eyes. She hugged the scrap of paper.

The father's last act was to give his daughter a priceless gift—reconciliation. In the face of death, both father and daughter were willing to forgive. When both realized that time on this earth is not unending, they were desperate to make things right.

The father's last act was to give his daughter a priceless gift— reconciliation.

Don't wait. You may not think a renewed relationship is even possible—at least not the relationship you hope for—but why not at least explore every possible avenue? Life is short.

Someday that daughter of yours (or, if you're a woman reading this book, that father of yours) who has been a thorn in your side is going to die. Of course, it's statistically more likely that you, the father, will die first. Since you know that day is coming, ask yourself, *Is there anything I need to say to my daughter? Any unfinished business I shouldn't put off any longer?*

Then don't put it off. Take care of it right now, or as soon as possible.

You and your daughter deserve the chance at reconciliation.

A Good Dad's Quick Reference Guide

- Say, "I'm sorry. Please forgive me."
- Make a plan for reconnecting.

NINE

Are You a Man or a Mouse? Squeak Up!

There's no higher compliment than, "I want to marry someone just like you, Dad." How to help your daughter get the kind of man you want her to have.

Flash back to when you were holding that little bundle of joy in your arms for the first time. You probably were terrified to hold her. She seemed so small and fragile that you were afraid you'd drop her and break her. That wave of protectiveness you felt nearly took your breath away.

Your daughter may be still in the womb, a newborn, a toddler, in elementary school, in middle school, or in high school, heading out the door for college, already entrenched in the workplace, or already a mom herself.

But no matter her stage in life, one thing never changes: every girl needs her daddy. What characteristics make the kind of dad that stands out from the rest? The kind of dad that captures his daughter's heart and builds a lifetime daddy-daughter connection?

Be There

When I asked my daughter Holly, now in her forties, what she remembers most about growing up in our home, she said, "It wasn't the organized activities. It was the spontaneous fun, the Huggy Hairy moments, that stand out."

My daughters' favorite game was Huggy Hairy and the Big Bad Wolf. I'd pretend I was a ferocious wolf, chase the girls around the room, "capture" them, and then put them in the "pot" (on the couch) to cook them. I'd sprinkle them with invisible salt, put in a few imaginary vegetables, and then say, "Oh no! I forgot the pepper!" I'd turn my back, and that was their cue to escape. Of course, then I'd return with the pepper and moan and groan as if I could never guess in a thousand years that they'd escape.

I didn't follow any game book or any script. I was simply there with them in the moment. When a father is present and active in the home, that presence provides assurance, safety, and comfort to his daughter. But only regularity can build that sense of belonging to the family that children crave. As we saw in the last chapter, that's why the "Stuff-y" dad, who uses gifts to replace his presence, and the In-N-Out dad, who thinks he can build a relationship with his daughter whenever he feels like it, will never be able to build the daddy-daughter connection his daughter longs for.

Dad, have you ever had your daughter say, "Please, Dad, don't show up for my game [or concert or other event]. It's embarrassing"? Well, don't fall for it.

My daughter Krissy tried that once, adding that it wasn't

"cool" to have your dad come and watch—or worse yet, cheer for you from the stands. But where my daughters are, I am, so I went anyway. Even though Krissy acknowledged me with only a slight lift of her left pinky, which was resting on her knee, the joy in her face told me all I needed to know. She really did want me there. Guys, your daughters will do early in life what all women do—lie like dogs. They don't mean to lie, but they do. What they tell you isn't always what they really mean, like the time my wife said, "Oh, we don't have to get dessert," so I drove on, only to see tears sliding down her face a few minutes later because we didn't stop for dessert.

You see, when you show up for your daughter's events, you're saying clearly, "You're important. You matter. What interests you interests me." I know you have a demanding schedule, juggling your job and your family. But when you are willing to put your own schedule aside to enter your daughter's life, that says everything about her value to you. It's the best defense you can give your daughter against the jerks and takers of the world.

Building a daddy-daughter connection doesn't happen all at once. It's all the little deposits of being there along the way. You might have heard the quote, "A woman's place is in the home." But this is also just as true: "A man's place is in the home."

Understand Her Instead of Trying to Fix Her

I learned the hard way that even psychologist dads shouldn't jump in with solutions.

One time at breakfast, Holly was talking about a problem she had. The solution was so obvious I couldn't believe my logical firstborn had missed it. So I spewed my wisdom all over her and waited for a pat on the back. Instead I was greeted with stony silence.

Finally Holly said, "Dad, you know what you ought to do?"

"What's that?"

"You ought to read your own books."

Ouch.

I'd pulled a typical father maneuver, running over her emotionally and telling her what to do instead of taking the time to enter her world. "Holly, I apologize. I was wrong."

One thing about firstborns—they can go for the jugular. I was a mess for hours after that.

We dads want to fix problems. But, Dad, your daughter doesn't want you to fix everything in her world. She only wants you to understand her. That means instead of jumping straight to an answer, as we males are prone to do, she needs you to listen to her process through the whole enchilada.

> Instead of jumping straight to an answer, as we males are prone to do, she needs you to listen to her process through the whole enchilada.

What shouldn't you say? "The answer is simple." Why? Because it isn't to her. This may not be your first rodeo with that situation, but it's hers. If you want to develop a child who has problem-solving skills of her own, you need to allow her to walk through it.

Instead of offering a solution, you need to show empathy. Whoa, there's a trait that's hard to come by for us males. But when you develop it, you'll be amazed at how it strengthens your daddy-daughter connection. "Honey, you really seem bothered by this. Why don't you tell me about it?"

Treat Your Wife as the Treasure She Is

Let me ask you something. When your house is a mess, who is the first one who notices—you or your wife? It's a biological fact that men are quite capable of walking past a heap of dishes in the sink and then going to bed and sleeping soundly. It's also a well-known fact that estrogen and dirty dishes don't mix. Nine out of ten women can't close their eyes if the kitchen isn't cleaned up.

How often do you get home from work before your wife and opt to clean the kitchen instead of putting your feet up in that La-Z-Boy? What would your wife do if you not only put the dirty dishes in the dishwasher but also actually wiped off the kitchen counters too? Imagine . . .

> Nine out of ten women can't close their eyes if the kitchen isn't cleaned up.

Your wife walks in, exhausted from her run-around day. Where she expects to see grime, she sees a sparkling clean kitchen. For some of you, your wife might need to walk outside to check the number on your house to make sure she hasn't inadvertently wandered into someone else's abode.

Most of all, your daughter is watching. What your girl sees in the way you treat your wife sets the bar for how she will expect her dates, and later, her husband, to treat her.

So take a look around your house. Then take a look at yourself.

Your daughter needs to see you treat your wife as someone special and worthy of respect. That's one of the reasons I never allowed my kids to mouth off to their mom. You shouldn't allow your daughter to either.

Believe in Your Daughter

A young woman named Elizabeth wanted to do something no girl had ever done in her hometown—run for the presidency of her high school.

"My father believed in me," Elizabeth explained. "I grew up feeling respected."[1]

Not only did John Van Hanford, Elizabeth's dad, instill in his daughter the belief that she could achieve great things, but because of his fathering style, Elizabeth found it easy to relate to men. "I grew up liking men because I liked my father, and it was apparent he liked himself."

It wasn't surprising, then, that Elizabeth made a wise choice for a husband—a man who served for years as a respected senator from Kansas and then presidential nominee from the Republican Party. "What I admire and respect [in my husband] is what I admired and respected in my dad," Elizabeth explained.[2]

Who did Elizabeth marry? A man by the name of Robert Dole. She went on to become secretary of transportation under the Reagan administration and also served as director of the American Red Cross. Today, women sit on the Supreme Court. They run businesses, have their own professional basketball league, win the World Cup in soccer, have growing categories of sports in the Olympics, and hold high positions in the military.

There are very few things a woman can't do. If your daughter wants to be a pilot and develops those skills, she can be a pilot. If she wants to be a CEO, she can be a CEO. Your daughter has as much of a chance to fulfill her dreams as your son does. But sometimes those dreams can come at the price of family relationships. You, Dad, can prepare your daughter to think critically about how the world works and how the job market works. If

your daughter wants to have a family someday and also have a career, she can learn to
be creative. The Internet and telecommuting
have changed the face of corporate America.
You can help her explore these family-
friendly ways to earn money.

> Believe in her.
> Encourage
> her dreams.
> And give her a
> well-balanced
> view of how the
> world works.

The most important things you can do
are what John Van Hanford did for his daughter: Believe in her. Encourage her dreams.
And give her a well-balanced view of how the
world works.

Allow Her to Hurt

The hardest thing a father can do is let his daughter hurt, but
sometimes pain is the only path to maturity. If your boy comes
home roughed up by a bully, your natural reaction is, "I'll teach
you how to hit him back . . . and win." If your daughter comes
home emotionally hurt by something a boy at school said, you
start thinking about the bazooka in the back of your closet.

This is a tough world. Life isn't always fair. Don't stunt your
daughter's maturity by always rushing in to save her. Sometimes
being a good dad means letting your daughter work her own way
out of a tight, even painful spot in the constant swirl of changing
emotions and relationships that girls face as they grow up. It isn't
easy, but it's essential in your daughter's development.

However, I'm not saying that you should ever allow your
daughter to be abused in any way by a peer or any adult in her
world. I'm talking about the everyday fine-tuning that happens
when girls brush shoulders with others in their world and need to

> Don't stunt your daughter's maturity by always rushing in to save her.

learn how to best deal with others, while at the same time standing up for themselves and doing the right thing.

Mei Li, a petite second-grader, was often picked on by Mark, the bully of her class. Her dad wanted to rush right in and fix things for her—with Mark, his parents, her teacher, and the school administration. But he also knew that, as a petite girl, she might end up facing off with a lot of bullies in her life and needed to learn how to deal with them.

Instead, he taught her three steps.

Step 1: When the bully does something to you, you face them eye-to-eye confidently and say, "Please do not do that again. I don't appreciate it."

Step 2: When the bully tries it again, you face them eye-to-eye and say with determination, "I asked you not to do that. I do not like it. If you do that again, I'll have to get the teacher involved."

Step 3: If the bully does it again, then you tell your teacher and get her involved. Your bully needs to know you mean business.

(By the way, the one thing her dad did do was inform the teacher quietly of the three steps he'd asked Mei Li to carry out, so that the teacher would know if Mei Li talked to her, the encounter with the bully was already on step 3.)

With these three steps, thirty-five-pound Mei Li was able to face down any bullies at school who threatened her. After all, bullies lack confidence, which is why they bully, to seem bigger on the outside than they feel on the inside. In fact, by the end of second grade, Mark said to her with admiration, "Wow, you're the toughest girl I know." By third grade, Mark had become Mei Li's champion, telling other kids not to mess with her or they'd have him to answer to.

To this day, Mei Li, now in eighth grade, is respected by all her classmates and faces the world with confidence. That dad did his daughter a favor when, instead of trying to solve her problems and lessen her hurt, he gave her tools with which to handle the situation.

To raise responsible daughters, you also have to allow them to feel a sting every once in a while. When one of my daughters started to whine about doing the dishes, I decided to nip the whine in the bud. I walked into the kitchen.

"Tonight, I'm doing your work," I said to her, taking the dish towel out of her hands. "Go and take care of whatever you want to do."

I chose my words carefully—"I'm doing your work." There wasn't a worse punishment I could give my daughter. I could see in her eyes that she felt guilty, and I wanted her to feel guilty.

I had barely put the last dish away when she walked tentatively into the kitchen again, looking lost. "I'm sorry I didn't do the dishes," she said in a meek voice.

"Do you understand why I was upset?"

"Yes," she said in a barely audible voice.

"When Mom and I ask you to do something around the house, we expect you to do it with a happy face. What kind of face did you have?"

She hung her head. "A pouting face."

I gave her a hug and affirmed her as a person, but the lesson was reinforced. She hurt, she grew, and she never whined about the dishes after that. In the Leman family, we all pitch in. That's because we have a home; we're not running a hotel.

The old adage is true: "No pain, no gain."

It's true in every area of life, including rearing your daughter.

A Daughter Needs a Dad Who . . .

- is honest and trustworthy.
- is even-tempered.
- gets behind her eyes to see her world.
- lovingly confronts.
- has a sense of humor.
- gives her the gift of positive expectations.
- cares and comforts.
- is full of grace and acceptance.
- communicates by talking and listening.
- makes her heart smile.

Teach Your Daughter That Others Matter

When my two older daughters were young, I befriended a man who worked at the gas station where I regularly filled my tank. He and his wife had little kids, and they had hit some hard times. When I learned about his story, I went home and told our family about it.

"They're going to have a tight Christmas," I said. "How can we help them?"

When I let the kids come to their own conclusion, somebody came up with the idea that they could donate some of their own toys for Christmas gifts. I made a point of reminding them that for something to really be a gift, they would need to consider giving away toys they really enjoyed, not just toys they never played with and knew that another child wouldn't either.

My oldest daughter, Holly, had two stuffed animals she treasured—a wolf named Lilac and a raccoon with Olympic circles on it that she'd received for her recent birthday. Suddenly, she clutched that raccoon with a new intensity. Finally she handed it to me. "You said we should give the best that we can—and raccoon and Lilac are my best."

The point hit home, and Lilac and the raccoon soon had a new home.

Dad, if you want your daughter to be happy, it's critical she think of others first. If she is focused only on herself, she'll always be frustrated because somebody will always be better than her and prettier than her. But a daughter who seeks to notice others first? She'll always be fulfilled in her life's missions, since so many people on this earth need to be noticed and appreciated. Her relationships will be rich and varied.

> If you want your daughter to be happy, it's critical she think of others first.

Because we Lemans focused on serving others, I see that same drive in each of my daughters and my son to this day. All five of our children are generous to the core.

Let me ask you a rubber-meets-the-road question, Dad: If you were to die tomorrow, what have you taught your daughter about serving others?

Robert F. Kennedy was assassinated when his daughter,

Kathleen, was only seventeen years old. But in the years he had with her, he prepared her for life. "My father believed in setting difficult courses for children because that made them stretch to become more. My father's credo was: Try . . . don't give up . . . win!"[3]

Kathleen Kennedy Townsend has spent most of her adult life in public service, including winning a seat as Maryland's first female lieutenant governor. As her state's second-ranking politician, Townsend developed the first statewide initiative in the nation that systematically targeted crime hotspots by pulling together previously scattered government agency operations—community policing, probation enforcement, nuisance abatement, youth violence prevention, and community mobilization.

Have you taught your daughter the importance of serving? Does she know that life is more fulfilling when she focuses on making a difference in her family, her community, her nation, and the world, rather than racing to the gym after work to try to fit her size-10 body into a size-4 dress? Does she understand the importance of persevering and refusing to give up? Have you taught her that sometimes sacrifice and service hurts? That at times we have to give up things we want in order to care for others' needs first? If so, you are preparing your daughter well for life outside the walls of your home.

Use Reality to Teach Life Lessons

"Daddy, do something!" Krissy said. Her eyes were frantic, and she was wringing her hands.

We were standing in a shopping center parking lot when we saw a man slap a woman across the face and then shove her into a car.

Before the words were even out of Krissy's mouth, I was already hurrying toward the man and woman. But he peeled out of the parking lot in his car and passed us. The woman's face was turned toward the window. She was sobbing.

When I made my way back to my young daughter, she was sobbing too. I hugged her. "Krissy, I wish you hadn't seen that, but you need to know something. There are men in this world who treat their wives like that all the time. They abuse women and hurt them." I paused, waiting for the words to sink in, so that she'd also hear my next words. "Honey, your job is to find a man who treats you with respect. One who will love you, care for you, and *never* hit you."

Krissy was silent on the drive home, her brain working on overdrive to process all she'd seen and heard. It was her first encounter with the harsh realities many women face in life due to sick, predatory men.

As much as we'd like to shield our daughters from the ugly realities of life, it's impossible. Bad things happen. The important thing is how you interpret the event for your daughter.

Often when our kids were growing up, we'd drive by an accident. A car would be rolled over, and police flares would be lighting up the sky. An ambulance would be nearby. I'd say out loud, "Bet it had to do with drugs or alcohol." Before long, my kids would speak up before I did. When we came upon an accident, one of them would say, "Think it was a druggie, Dad?" On purpose I imprinted my kids to connect drugs and alcohol with accidents and other unpleasant events.

> Bad things happen. The important thing is how you interpret the event for your daughter.

So many times we dads are so focused on trying to positively imprint our kids—with respect, career success, financial success, happiness, a good work ethic, and so on—that we forget to connect the dots for them on the negative parts of life. For example, if someone is irresponsible, lazy, and selfish, that often leads to tragedy, financial ruin, moral upheaval, and a host of other things.

It's true that tragedy strikes good and decent people. But tragedy for certain will follow irresponsible behavior. It's only a matter of time. If your daughter marries a violent man who cares only about himself and doesn't value women, eventually she will be abused.

That's why you cannot afford to be silent, Dad. Your daughter is looking up to you to help her determine how the world works. If you're not talking to her and assisting her with interpreting that, she'll be forced to guess and make her own way in life. Think back to when you were young. How much did you really know about the world? If you look back, what would you have changed, if only you'd have known differently? Do you really want your daughter making decisions now with no more knowledge than you had then? Scary thought, isn't it?

Real Men . . .

- show their emotions.
- share their emotions.
- are honest and forthright.
- love their children unconditionally.

Walk Your Talk

Imprinting on your daughter for a lifetime is only partially about what you say. It is even more influenced by what you do. Do you walk your talk? Does your daughter see love, kindness, stability, and a willingness to serve in your actions? Or does she see impatience, misplaced priorities, competition, and cheap shots?

Let's say your daughter has to write an essay for school on how a male should treat a female. If it were based on what she sees under your roof, what would that paper say?

If you're thinking, *Ouch,* then it's time for a big change in your behavior toward your family.

If you're thinking, *Hey, most of the time I do all right, but there are those times when I . . . ,* then think through how you'll respond in advance to "those times."

If you're thinking, *Hey, I'm pretty perfect,* then you need a bigger reality check than the rest of us dads. None of us is God, and we all need a little help now and again. That's what this book is all about.

Ask Dr. Leman

Q: My wife and I split up after twenty-two years of marriage, because my wife had an affair for the last eight years of it and refused to give it up, even when I begged her to and said I still loved her. We have four children—three boys and a girl— but our twenty-one-year-old college daughter is the one who's most devastated and caught in the middle. The three boys still live with me. When my daughter comes home to visit (my ex and I live in the same town still), her mom plans so many activities that I only get to see my daughter for a brief time. I really love my daughter, and I miss her. The two of us have always been close in heart and share a lot of interests. Her brothers miss her too. But she's not willing to go against my wife, who is very strong-willed and skillful at manipulating others.

I've confronted my ex, saying that it's only fair I get to spend time with my daughter and that she can't continue to manipulate Julia like that. But she throws it back in my face: "Well, if she wanted to spend time with you, she'd figure it out. That's not my problem!" Then she takes my daughter shopping, fills up her schedule even more, and pretends like they're best friends. Any suggestions? My daughter is too important to me to let this slide. We talk on the phone and e-mail a lot, but I feel like I'm on the outside looking in at my daughter's life, and I don't like it.

—Bill, Michigan

A: Wow, your ex is a real piece of work, and I'm amazed you hung in there with an affair for eight years. But it's clear to me what she's doing right now. She wants things to be like they were with her daughter—activities they did together—when you two were still married. But with a divorce, nothing is like it was. It's impossible to go backward and reclaim what you had. Your wife is stuck in a world of pretending that things between her and her daughter are hunky-dory, and life is as usual. From the picture you've painted of your ex, though, she wouldn't understand that right now, so you can only work on what's in your control.

Right now, you're walking a tightrope. You should never, ever badmouth your ex to your children. They'll figure out soon enough what the story is. If you badmouth her, your kids will turn her into Mother Teresa—trust me.

I suggest that you quietly arrange a time to see your daughter by yourself, even if that means spontaneously getting in the car and driving or flying to meet her at college. Tell her face to face, "Julia, I love spending time with you, and I miss that. I know you want to see me too. But it seems like when you come to visit, your mom has the whole time mapped out for you. How do you feel about that?"

From what you've said of your daughter, it sounds like she'll likely say, "I don't like it. I miss time with you."

Then you gently say, "Julia, you're now twenty-one. Within a year, you'll be graduating from college. You're no longer a little girl. You need to stand firm about what you want. Honey, I know you love your mother, but she doesn't own you like a piece of property. When you come home, you should be the one arranging your schedule, not her. Then it will be your choice who you spend time with, how much time, and when. You owe that to yourself. So I guess you have a decision to make. You can live the rest of your life being ruled by your mother, or decide to take charge of your own life."

With that said, you don't push the subject further. You've planted the seed. The next actions are up to your daughter.

My heart goes out to you. But in the meantime, keep loving that daughter and engaging in her life however you can. Within the next year, as she graduates, her life will change again. She'll need all the encouragement and affirmation she can get from you, with a toxic parent on the other side of her.

"You Can't Handle the Truth!"

In the movie *A Few Good Men,* Tom Cruise plays Lieutenant Daniel Kaffee, a military prosecutor who is going after the ice-cold Colonel Nathan R. Jessup, played by Jack Nicholson. When the case seems all but lost, the young prosecutor sets up the caustic colonel and triggers his anger so that at last he blurts out the truth—that he *did* order the Code Red that killed Santiago, a soldier.

Well, Dad, this is when the rubber meets the road. Can you handle the truth? Take a look at the list of "good dad" qualities we talked about in this chapter. Put a little checkmark by ones where you say, "Hey, I'm doing pretty well in that area." Highlight or write on another sheet of paper the ones you need to work on.

If you take on the "good dad" qualities list to fine-tune your character, I've got news for you. You won't hit 100 percent on any of them. You'll fall short. You'll make mistakes. All of us do. But keep in mind that your goal isn't to be a *perfect* dad. There's no such thing on this earth. It's to be a *good* dad. Being a good dad isn't about buying your kids things or checking slick strategies off your to-do list. It's about relating to your daughter—taking the time to engage emotionally with your daughter in her world. When all is said and done, how are you doing with that?

I had a heartwarming conversation recently with a father of two teenage daughters. That tough guy brushed away tears as he told me, "I've always tried to be a good dad, but sometimes I wonder if I'm making enough of a difference in my girls' lives. Last week my older daughter, Michelle, broke up with her boyfriend. They'd been dating a year, and I was really nervous about the guy. I wasn't comfortable with how he treated her. Know what she told me? 'I want to marry someone just like you, Dad, and I realized Jake wasn't even close.' Wow."

There's no higher compliment a dad can receive than that.

Would you want your little girl to spend her life with somebody just like you?

If so, give yourself an A+, a pat on the back, and go out and celebrate with your daughter.

If not, it's time to change a few things about yourself—for your daughter's sake.

Are you a man, or a mouse? Squeak up!

A Good Dad's Quick Reference Guide

- Walk your talk.
- Become the kind of man you'd want your daughter to marry.

TEN

If You See a Turtle on a Fencepost . . .

. . . you'll know that critter didn't get there by itself. Why your daughter needs your encouragement to succeed in life.

I don't like to admit this publicly, but I've sat through the *Bachelorette* series and watched HGTV, cooking shows, and *Project Runway* with my wife and daughters. But I did it for one reason: as a man, I have to be interested in things that people I love care about. In fact, if they don't know that I care, they won't care what I know.

The day your daughter walks out the door of your home will come far more swiftly than you can ever imagine. I have ushered all four of my daughters out the door to college and have already escorted three of those daughters down the aisle to wedded bliss. It all happened in the blink of an eye.

Step into Your Daughter's World

Think back a few years, to when you first went to the dentist as a young kid. You hopped up to sit on the very edge of those uncomfortable waiting-room chairs, and your feet dangled. They were nearly numb, as much as you wiggled them, before your name was called. Then you climbed up the mountain of that strange chair and glimpsed all the shiny metal contraptions resembling torture devices from your nightmares. While you waited, you squeezed your eyes shut, imagining that dentist drill or shot coming your direction . . . closer, closer . . . and lived in terror of the moment.

The world can be a big, scary, confusing place when you're young.

Voices are constantly calling out to your daughter—teachers with different values than yours, teen blogs, YouTube snippets that flaunt sexy poses, and music videos that highlight the short shelf life of relationships, "romance" (all in the guise of sex), and marriage. Kids left on their own don't have the experience or maturity to adequately filter these voices.

When Hannah was seven years old, she had a toy computer that "talked" to her in simple, prerecorded language: "Welcome. Please select a category now."

One day, two-year-old Lauren turned it on.

This is gonna be good, I mused, curious to see what Lauren would do with a talking box.

"Welcome," the computer said. "Please select a category now."

Lauren didn't know what to do, so she just sat there. After fifteen seconds or so, the computer said again, "Please select a category now."

Lauren sighed in exasperation. Cupping her hands around

her mouth, she bent down toward the computer and called out, "Lady, I'm only two years old."

As those voices of life surround your daughter, she needs the benefit of your wisdom and past experiences to avoid many of the mistakes you may have made in life. That's why when divorced dads tell me, "I don't talk to my daughter about relationships. After all, what do I have to say? My own marriage failed," I have a blunt comeback.

"That's exactly the reason you *should* say something to your daughter—so she'll avoid making the same mistakes you and your ex did in your relationship."

No, you can't fix everything in your daughter's life, and you shouldn't. She needs room to grow, learn, and make her own mistakes along the way to hone her character. Not allowing her to make her own decisions, making excuses for her, and snowplowing her roads of life will only result in a weak-willed, wishy-washy adult who thinks everyone exists in this world to serve her. No daughter should be reared to be the center of the universe. But she does need to feel prized, appreciated, and an important part of your family.

If you can walk away with only one thought from this book, let it be this: what your daughter thinks of herself and the way the world works has everything to do with you, Dad. If you haven't taught her by your words and actions what's important in life and how valuable she is as a unique human being, she'll become whoever she thinks she's supposed to be to fit in with her peers.

But a girl who has been loved and cared for by her father in a close daddy-daughter connection will be equipped to say no to a

> What your daughter thinks of herself and the way the world works has everything to do with you, Dad.

peer group who demands, "Hey, be like us." Her response in her heart? *Why should I? My daddy says I should be myself. He loves me, he's there for me, and he likes who I am, just as I am.* There is no better antidote to peer pressure than a father's continual affirmation and active presence.

Stop right there. Note that I used the word *continual*. We guys can tend to be list checkers. "Okay, got the 'marriage' job done. Check." Or, "Yup, got the 'encourage the daughter' job done. Check." But fatherly affirmation doesn't come in one big "I'm proud of you" speech, after which you heave a sigh of relief, get your man-card back, and then whistle happily as you walk away into the wild blue yonder. The affirmation comes in lots of little ways over the years of your relationship.

Here are a couple of examples from my relationship with my second daughter, Krissy.

If it were left up to us males to remember birthdays, anniversaries, and any other important days, I'm convinced there wouldn't be nearly as many celebrations on this earth. Usually we guys leave those up to the females of the family, whom we assume are more naturally programmed to deal with those sorts of events. But I decided early on in my parenting that I wanted to be an engaged dad with my girls, not merely a dad who always passed the buck to his wife to sign cards and buy presents on behalf of both of us.

Funny thing: when Krissy married, she told me one of the things she remembered most clearly about growing up was that I signed many of her birthday cards instead of Sande.

Daughters notice these things, Dad. Don't think they don't. Little things matter, especially to the females in your life.

Krissy also remembers that, on her thirteenth birthday, I

went to a jewelry store and designed an amethyst ring for her. To this day, she still has it. It's the gift from her childhood she says she cherishes most because it took initiative on my part to pick it out, design it, and purchase it. Would I have been more comfortable with my artsy wife doing it? You bet! But being a good dad means stepping outside your comfort zone for the sake of your daughter.

The day will come when your daughter's personality, character qualities, and affections will be formed. When that day comes, what memories do you want her to have of her daddy?

Shortly after she moved to college, Krissy wrote Sande a letter that included these words:

> You and Dad have taught me so much. If it wasn't for your guidance, love, and discipline, I would never make it here at college. The morals you have taught me are now the characteristics I cling to, especially now that I'm on my own.

There's nothing better than finding out, when a daughter is grown, that she has internalized the values you've taught over the years and has chosen to live by them. That's what I mean by "the indelible imprint" of a father.

Dad, your daughter needs your help to gain confidence as she grows into a woman and to find her unique role in the world. That means she needs you to be interested in what she's interested in, at the time she's interested in it. Your daughter won't be interested in the same things when she's five as she will when she's fifteen. You have to go with the flow as her life and interests change. But what she needs most will stay consistent—your encouragement.

Learning How to Connect

My dad was a great provider, but he was the strong, silent type. We kids rarely interacted with him, except at the dinner table, where every night he asked each of us how our day went. We mainly reported events and didn't get into any touchy-feely stuff. I know my dad loved me, but he never spoke the words.

A month ago my wife and I attended a seminar of yours at a nearby church. You talked about "connecting with your daughter's heart." That phrase was like learning a new language, since I grew up in a family of four boys and now I have four girls, ages two through six. (Yeah, God has a sense of humor.) That thought sparked a lot of discussion between my wife and me. As crazy as it may sound, we had to brainstorm ways for me to connect with my daughters, because you're right—I did tend to parent the way my dad parented me, leaving the rearing of the girls up to my wife.

A lot has changed in the last three weeks. I used to come in the door quietly after work and try to escape straight to our bedroom to take a shower and wash my workday out of my head. Now when I come in the door, I make a great show of closing the door and calling dramatically, "Daddy's home!" All four girls rush to the door screaming, "Daddy!" and wrap themselves around my legs. Then I shuffle my way with four extra appendages into the kitchen to give my wife a big smooch, which always brings a loud "yuck" from my oldest daughter. It's now an everyday tradition. Hey, there's nothing like being greeted by five adoring females to boost a guy's ego! I'm learning to enjoy the cuddles and view the world through their eyes. Now I also read to them for an hour after dinner so my wife can have some quiet time. *Then* I finally get my shower.

Last night, Melody, our five-year-old, was sitting on my lap as I was reading. She turned around, reached up, and grabbed my face. Her blue eyes stared into mine. "Daddy, you're d'frent," she said.

Yes, this daddy is "d'frent."

—Kurt, Wisconsin

That Little Nudge of Encouragement

If you see a turtle on a fencepost, you know that critter didn't get there on its own. It had a little nudging . . . or a lot of nudging . . . to attain its lofty position. In the same way, your daughter needs nudges of encouragement in order to be motivated to rise to the top of the fencepost.

Do you have any idea how powerful these two words are: *Good job*?

What are you really saying? A bucket load: "Wow, you went after that difficult science project and gave it your all, even though that subject is hard for you. That speaks mountains to me about your character and determination. Those are the kind of qualities that will set you up for a lifetime." We men, who sometimes struggle to get out more than a grunt, need to

> Do you have any idea how powerful these two words are: *Good job?*

remember how significant even a few words can be to the person on the hearing end of them.

How about trying, "Wow, that has to make you feel good inside," after your daughter has learned a new soccer technique or memorized a piano piece for a recital?

But notice what I'm not saying: "I'm so proud of you. You're the best (soccer player/ musician) *ever!*" That would be blowing smoke, since there is always someone in the world who will be better.

The other day I saw a three-year-old boy with a Mohawk. The mother cooed, "Oh, Ethan, don't you look cool in that haircut— the coolest little boy I ever saw." That's false praise, and not even a three-year-old is stupid enough to fall for it. I turned the corner and saw a five-year-old girl with the collar turned up on her polo shirt. She was walking with a man who appeared to be her father. He, too, had the collar turned up on his polo shirt. Like father, like daughter. In the same way, many parents treat their children like trophies to show off, lauding their own parental accomplishments rather than rearing children to become capable, giving adults.

Our job is not to create look-alikes of ourselves or perfect models. Our job is to encourage the individual skills and talents of each of our daughters.

So the next time your daughter comes home with a report card, don't say, "Wow, you're so smart. Check out that A!" Instead, say, "Wow. You've worked so hard to pull your grade up in math. That B+ must make your heart smile. Great job!" That's effective encouragement that will keep your turtle motoring onward and upward.

FATHER

Free her
Affirm her
Trust her
Hold her
Encourage her
Role-model life for her

Simply stated, there's a big difference between *praise* and *encouragement*.

Praise focuses on the *person*. "Oh, Katherine, you're the cutest girl ever!"

Encouragement focuses on the *act*. "Katherine, I've noticed that you work hard to always look nice. I appreciate that effort, and your mother told me it makes her smile all over too." What does your daughter take from those few words? *Wow, my dad notices. And cool, it makes my mom feel good too. Even better, the two of them talked about me in a really great way.*

Dad, you just used the wonderful technique of "good gossip"—passing along something nice that someone else said about your daughter. It packs a powerful punch. Think about it. If a coworker told you that your boss said you were doing a great job and he was impressed, wouldn't that make you feel good? Wouldn't you work a little harder that day? Wouldn't the sun shine a little brighter when you popped outside for your lunch break?

Now, let me ask you: How many minutes did that take out of your day? If you talk fast, bet it was under a minute. You've

> Your daughter doesn't care what you know until she knows you care.

still got 1,439 minutes left to spend in your day! But most likely, nothing else you do or say that day will have the long-term impact of that one minute with your daughter.

Little nudges take only a moment but last a lifetime.

Your daughter doesn't care what you know until she knows you care.

A few words, a simple arm around the shoulder, a hug, a "good job," a note—all those little things stack up to a mountain of encouragement in your daughter's life.

Grace-Based Fathering

Shelli was a responsible eleven-year-old. She always kept track of her homework and whatever else she needed to bring to school. But during the first week of sixth grade everything fell apart. One day, Shelli left her lunch sitting on the counter at home. The next day, she forgot her math homework. The day after that, she only brought two of the three items for her science project. Her dad, Matt, is a firstborn and precise to the extreme. I don't think the guy ever walks out of his door without his suit on and every hair slicked down. But since his wife was traveling for her company, Matt was the one who got the SOS calls from his daughter. To say he was annoyed was an understatement. When Matt was at work as the CEO, he was at work, and no one interrupted him. But he also had a smart assistant who pointed out to him what was most important—that he retain his relationship with his daughter.

When he cooled down, Matt realized that his daughter was in one of the biggest transitions of her life. She was entering middle school, where she had not one classroom but a different room and requirements for every subject. No wonder the kid was off kilter. She was juggling a lot. It reminded him of when he first became CEO of the engineering firm, and he constantly felt overwhelmed by the responsibilities. That afternoon, when he picked her up from school, he had a discussion with Shelli quite different from the "hammering her for dropping the ball" one he'd planned earlier in the day.

"Middle school is sure different, isn't it, Shell? So much to keep track of . . . ," he said casually while they were driving home.

She slumped in the seat and nodded. "Yeah. It's hard."

"Kinda reminds me of when I first became CEO, when you were in third grade. There was so much to do, and I always felt like I was dropping the ball at home and at work. And sometimes I did."

Shelli sat up, looking startled. "You did?"

"Sure I did. Nobody is perfect, and I'm certainly not."

She was quiet a minute, then simply said, "Wow."

Matt plunged on. "One of the things that helped me was brainstorming with a guy I trusted how to make it all work. *Mmm*, maybe you and I could brainstorm. Is there anything that might make it easier for you with all the things going on in middle school?" he prompted.

She looked surprised. "Uh, well, I've been thinking . . . if I had one of those erasable boards with the weeks and days marked, so I could write on it, that would help."

He smiled. "Sounds like a plan. Want to stop by Office Depot? It's right on the way home. You can pick out whatever you want, and I'll spring for it. Anything for my girl."

Now, think how different that conversation could have turned out if Matt had gone with his first gut and spouted off, telling his daughter what a loser she was for not remembering things.

| Sometimes what your daughter needs most is for you to give her a break. |

Everyone makes mistakes. Everyone struggles with transitions. Sometimes what your daughter needs most is for you to give her a break.

It's called grace-based parenting. Your daughter forgets an important book at school, and you drive her back to pick it up. Do you do that all the time? No, because children need to be held accountable for their actions. That's the best way to learn, even though the process can be painful. But sometimes you need to give each other grace and room to maneuver. Think about the times you've blown your top and said something you wish you hadn't to your daughter, and she's forgiven you. Now that's grace—getting something you don't deserve. Shouldn't she be able to count on the same thing from you when she has a single bad day, or several in a row?

Combating Perfectionism

Of all the people on the planet, young women are the ones who understand more than anyone the toll perfectionism can take. The drive to always be right, always be pretty, always be smart, always be popular, and always be perfect has wreaked more havoc on the female population than anything else I know. It's led to anorexia, bulimia, depression, and suicide attempts, among other things.

The margin of error for females today is way too narrow. If she gains five pounds while in a growth spurt, she'll moan to her friends, "I'm getting fat." If she gets solid Bs on her report card, she'll compare with someone who got mostly As and think, *I'm so dumb.* If she doesn't get asked to the homecoming dance, she'll think she's ugly and that no one likes her. Girls tend to amplify their own shortcomings and assume that others somehow walk on a perfect cloud. But even supermodels have morning breath and get hair tangles, and somebody has to apply their makeup in the right way to enhance their natural features. Nobody dares to put their picture on a magazine until they've been worked over. Even then, the final is airbrushed to perfection. Yet the majority of teenage girls still compare themselves against this impossible standard in regard to beauty.

That's why it's critical, Dad, that you accept your daughter *as she is.* She needs a male to adore her, affirm her, relate to her, and build her up regardless of whether she's a klutz, she wears size-12 jeans in a high school teeming with size-6 bodies, or she's the "plain Jane" among her bunch of friends. Every girl longs to be seen for who she is, accepted for who she is, and valued for who she is. It's one of the reasons the music video "You Belong with Me" by Taylor Swift became an almost instant hit with girls ages eight and up across the nation. Girls who are more "plain Jane" could now dream of the day when that sweet, handsome boy at school would look beyond their simple T-shirts and sneakers, see the treasures they are, and realize, *What I've been looking for has been here the whole time.* Then that sweet, handsome boy would, of course, throw over that cheerleader girlfriend and decide, "You Belong with Me."[1]

> The margin of error for females today is way too narrow.

Contrast that with one of Taylor Swift's later videos, "I Knew You Were Trouble," which describes a girl who was attracted to the wrong kind of guy and, as a result, "lost her balance." The comment at the end of the video is cryptic: "I don't know if you know who you are until you lose who you are."[2]

Does your daughter know who she is? What kind of reflection does she see of herself in her daddy's eyes? Does she know she always belongs with you and that you never consider her to be average? That you prize and appreciate her?

That's why my friend Evan said to his high school freshman daughter on the first week of school, "Wow, great job putting that outfit together. You look really artsy—just like you. That oughta make some boys' heads turn at school," and he winked at her.

Of course, he got the signature teenage girl line: "D-a-a-a-a-d!" But inside she was thinking, *Cool. I look good. My dad thinks I look good. Maybe other boys will too.* And for a girl entering high school, that gave her the confidence boost she needed to step into new territory with her head held high.

Smart dad. A girl like that isn't going to fall for any lame line from a lust-ridden senior.

What can a dad do to help his daughter in such a perfectionistic world?

Teach Her How to Fail . . . Well

I want my daughters to know that my acceptance is unconditional. Succeed or fail, I'll love each of them the same. My love and acceptance aren't based on them being the prettiest, the most athletic, the most charming, the smartest, and certainly not the thinnest girls around. All I ask is that, whatever they decide to do, they give it their best shot. If they succeed, wonderful. If they fail, they can fail well. By that, I mean they can do so with a good attitude and evaluate what they've learned along the way.

Does your daughter have freedom to fail? Or do you expect her always to win? Does she feel your unconditional love, no matter what happens? Or is there disappointment, verbal or unspoken, that crushes her? Sadly, too many girls write themselves off as failures because they never quite "made it" in their daddy's eyes. They saw or felt his judgment, disappointment, and criticism, and they internalized the mantra that they have nothing to offer the world. They couldn't be more wrong.

We're all imperfect. No one can bat a hundred out of a hundred every time. But take a look around. God Almighty is using a lot of imperfect people to make positive marks on this planet.

> Does your daughter have freedom to fail? Or do you expect her always to win?

Thomas Edison didn't get the light bulb right the first time. He had to fail, and fail, and fail—in fact, more than one thousand times—before he succeeded. Many people thought Thomas Edison's elevator didn't go all the way to the top, and that Albert Einstein, who developed the theory of relativity, was a few fries short of a Happy Meal. A lot of other brilliant people have also been written off.

Even the basketball great Michael Jordan experienced his share of failure. As he says, "I've missed more than 9,000 shots in my career. I've lost almost 300 games. 26 times I've been trusted to take the game winning shot and missed. I've failed over and over and over again in my life. And that is why I succeed."[3]

Your daughter deserves the same opportunity to fail, so that later she might succeed. Others might write her off, but if her daddy believes in her, she can still fly high.

What Failure Really Is

"Only those who dare to fail greatly can
achieve greatly."—Robert F. Kennedy

"Ever tried. Ever failed. No matter. Try again.
Fail again. Fail better."—Samuel Beckett

"Failure provides the opportunity to begin
again, more intelligently."—Henry Ford

"Every strike is closer to the next
home run."—Babe Ruth

Flaunt Your Failures

If you want your daughter to handle her failures well, you
better 'fess up about your own. Telling your daughter stories
about yourself and the goofy, zany, and stupid things you've done
in life is not only entertaining and fun; it's a great way to take the
pressure off your daughter's internal self-talk. This is especially
important to firstborn and only-born daughters who may tend to
be perfectionistic and uptight, thinking they have to do things
exactly right to please Dad.

Many of us dads work hard to stay perched on our pedestals.
Frankly, it's one of the most damaging things you can do as a dad.
After all, if your daughter never sees how you handle failure, how
can she learn to deal positively with her own?

I honestly believe that one of the reasons my books have done
so well and why I've been asked to appear on so many national

television shows is that I'm not your typical shrink. If you passed me on the street and didn't know who I was, you'd never guess I was a professional psychologist. When I talk to people, I'm a regular guy. I share my failures, as well as the things I've learned along the way.

The same principle works in parenting. Are you a regular guy with your kids? Or do you try too hard to be perfect in their eyes?

Thirteen-year-old Jane threw down her pencil. "I'm stupid," she told her dad. "Everybody else gets math, but I can't get it. No matter how hard I try." She burst into tears, ran to her room, and slammed the bedroom door shut.

Her dad, Alan, could relate more than she knew. With a little digging in their basement, he came up with a wad of old papers and knocked on her door. "I thought you might like to see these," he said and handed them to her. They were math papers and tests from his seventh-grade year, with red Fs and Ds emblazoned all over them.

His daughter stared at them in shock.

"I understand your frustration more than you may think," he said quietly, then left the papers with her in her room.

About an hour later, his daughter walked into his home office. "Uh, Dad, how did you handle not being good at math? I mean, you do stuff with it now for your job, right?"

Alan was able to share with his daughter how he'd felt stupid and like a failure all the way until his sophomore year of high school, when he finally had a teacher who pulled him aside and quietly worked with him for an hour after school each day to catch him up on the basics of math principles he'd somehow missed.

"Honey, you're not stupid," he explained. "Some of us just have to work a little harder in certain subjects. Guess you inherited your math gene from your dad. Sorry!" He grinned. "But the good thing is, now that I know how you're feeling, we can work out a plan for getting you some help."

"Thanks, Dad!"

When you flaunt your failures, your daughter's failures are put in a more realistic perspective. And if you need to seek answers, you can seek them together, without her feeling stupid or like a failure.

Practice Saying "I'm Sorry," and Say It Often

I'm a behavioral psychologist, so you'd think I, of all people, would know how to navigate my daughters and their emotions without wreaking havoc on the female population in my house. But sometimes I do it very wrong and have to say two of the hardest words for men to say—"I'm sorry."

One morning, three-year-old Lauren was holding a biscuit in front of our dog, Barkley, and calling in a singsong voice, "Barkley, want a treat, want a treat? Barkley, want a treat, want a treat?"

Krissy and I thought Lauren looked so cute doing it that we called out the same thing to Lauren. "Lauren, want a treat, want a treat? Lauren, want a treat, want a treat?"

Without saying a word, Lauren slid off her stool and left the room.

"Uh-oh," Krissy said. "I don't think that went over very well."

I walked into the next room and watched as Lauren gave me "the Look"—the same one my wife shoots me when I'm in big, big trouble. As I came closer to Lauren, she backed away and slowly stepped toward the stairs. I took one step forward; she took one step back. The process continued until she was at the landing. Then she slid on her stomach all the way down the stairs and fled into her downstairs bedroom, locking her door.

Krissy, being the peacemaker she is, tried talking to Lauren through the door. "We weren't making fun of you. We thought you looked so cute and adorable, that's all."

With the tone that only an aggrieved child can muster, Lauren firmly announced, "You need to apologize."

"I'm really sorry, Lauren. Honest, I am."

"No, you need to write it down."

> Lauren gave me "the Look"—the same one my wife shoots me when I'm in big, big trouble.

Keep in mind, Lauren was only three years old. She couldn't even read yet, but Krissy dutifully obeyed.

Even so, Lauren still wouldn't open the door. "Daddy needs to apologize too," she said through the still-locked door.

I came downstairs and said my piece, but attorney Lauren repeated the same thing to me. "You need to write it down too."

I took out a piece of paper and wrote: *Lauren, I am very, very sorry. I love you. Daddy.*

Only after the two apologies were slipped under the door was Lauren willing to exit her room and relate face-to-face with each of us again.

Now, I'm the kind of guy who has to have his wife tell him the difference between a monkey wrench and a crescent wrench. I also can't tell a carburetor from a starter. But one of the things I'm very, very good at—I should be, I've had lots of practice—is saying "I'm sorry" to my family members. I'm living proof that those two words are essential and powerful in establishing a trust relationship between a father and a daughter.

There are times when I haven't even realized I hurt one of my daughters until after the fact. Then "the Look" told me instantly I was in trouble. But as soon as I reflected on the incident, I would immediately apologize. It's amazing how a simple apology can melt away a daughter's defiance and improve your relationship.

If it's particularly difficult for you to utter these words, practice saying the phrase the next time you're shaving. Start out with, "I'm . . ." and give yourself a ten-second pause. Then say, ". . . sorry." The next time, cut the pause down to eight seconds, then six seconds, then four, then string the two words together. "I'm sorry," spoken quickly, will be one of the most valuable tools you'll ever learn to use as a dad.

Reveal Your Embarrassing Moments

All of us have embarrassing moments. They're a part of life. Learning how to handle them is critical in your daughter's battle against perfectionism. You can start by revealing some of your own.

"Kids, you won't believe what I did," I told my daughters after I'd completed a segment on Geraldo Rivera's show. I explained that after the show his wife, CeCe, her parents, and I were standing in his dressing room, discussing what I'd shared about parenting. CeCe was intrigued by it.

When Geraldo arrived, I could see the first thing that flickered across his face: *I thought we finished with this guy. Why's he hanging around?*

"What happened next, Dad?" my kids wanted to know.

"Then I knocked Geraldo's beer onto the floor."

"No!"

"Yes. It broke and spilled all over the place."

> "Kids, you won't believe what I did."

They laughed so hard I thought they'd need to make an emergency trip to the bathroom. "Really?" they squealed. "You knocked Geraldo's beer to the floor in his dressing room?"

"Darn right I did. It was a Heineken."

Our family had a good laugh. "I can't believe you knocked over Geraldo Rivera's beer," they kept saying.

Why did I share this embarrassing story with my kids? Because middle school and high school—even grade school—kids often live in intense fear of being embarrassed. The worst thing that can happen to them, in many of their minds, is to be laughed at or to do something dumb. This is especially true of daughters. Their fragile psyches can be rocked for weeks over one remark.

That's why I make it a practice to let my kids know about situations where I looked really bad. There I was, in a celebrity's dressing room, and what did suave Dr. Leman do? He knocked the television host's beer onto the floor!

So, Dad, tell them your stories. Don't hold back on any of the self-incriminating details. It's great therapy for kids to be able to laugh along with their parents. It models for them that it's not only okay for us to laugh at ourselves—it's a healthy response to embarrassing moments.

My kids know all about my foibles, including the fact that I am claustrophobic and have to sit in the front-row seat of an airplane or this weird feeling starts to tap-dance its way up my back, and I get downright panicky.

Everyone fails at times and has embarrassing moments. Understanding those realities and having them modeled by their dad, the male role model they respect the most, goes a long way toward putting those events in proper perspective when they do happen.

So I spilled Rivera's beer on the floor. Still, life amazingly continued on with barely a ripple.

Don't Measure Her Success by Her Achievements

When Holly first went away to college, our firstborn, straight-A student started pulling all Cs. Years later, when someone asked her how I responded, she said, "Dad didn't overreact. His attitude was more, 'They're your grades and it's your life; if these grades aren't good enough, you'll either bear the consequences or get the rewards.'"

Throughout their schooling, I imprinted my daughters with the value of a good education. But I never led them to believe that grades were all that mattered. In fact, I sometimes went overboard in the other direction. When our kids got their report cards, they knew I paid more attention to the teacher's written character comments than I did to the actual grades. I wanted my daughters to know that what matters in the long run is the type of person you are, not the things you do.

> What matters in the long run is the type of person you are, not the things you do.

But how many families spend every day of the week running from school to soccer, Girl Scouts, karate, music lessons, and who knows what else—all in the name of giving their kids a leg up on life? Are we so addicted to achievement that we're willing to run ourselves and our children ragged to do it?

I know some three- and four-year-olds who are involved in four or more activities outside the home every week. Is that really good for a young child? No.

Is it okay for your high schooler to be so involved in after-school activities that you barely see her from freshman year to senior year, except when she's putting her hand out for the car keys? No, it's not.

Sadly, we live in a society that rates achievement by how busy we are and how much we can get done. But is life truly all about running from place to place? If you're rating your daughter's achievement by how much she's involved in, why would you expect her to do any different when she marries and your grand-kids enter the picture? And are you likely to ever see her and your grandkids at your home for Christmas dinner?

Frenetic activity says one thing to your daughter: "Prove yourself." Is that really what you want her to believe? That who she is right now isn't good enough or valuable enough? That she has to continually run from place to place to prove her worth?

To build a lifelong, healthy daddy-daughter connection, focus on spending time together rather than on getting caught in the activity trap. Go out of your way to prove your love. Prove your commitment. Prove your affection. To a daughter, they're all spelled out in one word: *time*.

A Good Dad's Quick Reference Guide

- Affirm your daughter for who she is now.
- Give her freedom both to fail and to fly.

ELEVEN

Time Is Tickin'

Your girl will grow faster than a speeding bullet. How to handle the transitions and fine-tune your priorities.

L ife is full of transitions, and with daughters whose ages span three decades, I've come to realize that, as a dad, I won't like all of those changes. But that doesn't mean they won't come. There's a toe-tapping DC Talk song that includes the lyrics "Time is tickin' away, tick tick tickin' away."[1] Isn't that the truth? The older I get, the faster time seems to tick away. Funny how that is.

Someday that baby you held in your arms will start to walk. Then she'll run . . . down the hallway, squealing as you chase her.

She'll have her first dance with you in the kitchen as she stands on your toes and you move your feet.

She'll head off to kindergarten with a tiny pink backpack with her favorite cartoon character imprinted on it. You'll mop up your wife's tears—and your own—when you drop her off for her first full day of school.

She'll face her first bully on the playground, and you'll want to clean the kid's clock.

She'll get her first bad grade on a test, and she'll cry.

She'll get a training bra . . . enough said.

She'll have her first crush . . . and get her heart broken.

She'll wobble out the door in her first pair of high heels.

The next thing you know, she'll be headed off to prom with a boy who is giving her that Bullwinkle look you remember so well from your own adolescent years.

She'll get her first kiss from a non–relative who is of the male gender. She may get a lot more if you're not the dad she needs you to be.

Then, before you know it, she'll be applying to colleges and packing her bags.

Her First Night Not Under My Roof

My heart was about ripped out of my chest as Sande and I made the drive to college with our firstborn daughter, Holly, and all her dorm stuff in tow. The unloading of it at the school went far too swiftly, with the help of eager college boys who seemed to be casting enough side glances at Holly to risk neck problems the rest of their lives.

> *Would strangling a college boy be considered self-defense?* I wondered briefly.

Would strangling a college boy be considered self-defense? I wondered briefly.

After a full day of meetings, touring campus, and helping Holly set up the rooms, I announced, "Well, we'd better get going."

My wife, Sande, shot me the look that means, *Don't mess with me, buddy boy.* "We can't leave yet. I haven't made Holly's bed."

Keep in mind this was college, not

preschool. But when your wife shoots you that kind of look, you'd better back off if you know what's good for you.

Five minutes later, with the bed made, there were no more excuses. For the first time in almost twenty years, one of our kids would sleep under a different roof. I could hardly take it. Neither could my wife, but she handled the transition differently.

I watched Sande hug and rock our eighteen-year-old, as if wanting one final moment with her little baby. As for me, I kept my distance. I knew if I didn't, I'd break down on the spot. What guy wants to be a blubbering idiot in public?

Holly took a step toward me. She put her arms around me and said, "I love you, Dad."

That did it. I started sobbing . . . profusely.

As I held my daughter in the parking lot at college that day, I wondered where the time had gone. I remembered when she was only 20.5 inches long, and we brought her home from the hospital. I didn't want her to be cold so I turned up the heat so high we could have popped popcorn in the sink. I checked every ten minutes to make sure she was breathing. Then, when she was ten years old, I stepped on something in my bathroom. It appeared to be a bra, so I assumed it belonged to my wife, yet it clearly was much too small for Sande. In amazement and great curiosity, I carried that thing around the corner and called out to Sande, "Honey, what's this?"

"That's Holly's bra."

My Holly has a bra? I mused, then chuckled. "This looks like it's going to grow up someday and become a bra."

Now the same Holly was grown up enough to go to college. I wasn't ready to wake up on Saturday mornings and not see her in front of her cereal bowl. Would anybody else eat Cocoa Puffs? Or would they go stale? Funny how strange your thoughts can become when you're emotionally overwhelmed.

Somehow, in the midst of the haze, my testosterone kicked in, and I made a swift exit after asking her to call us that night. I pointed our car back toward home and, by some miracle, we got there safely. I don't even remember the drive. That night I lived for Holly's phone call. When the phone rang, I nearly tackled everyone trying to get to it first. But the call was for her sister.

> Funny how strange your thoughts can become when you're emotionally overwhelmed.

Seven days later, Holly finally called and rambled on about freshman week.

Finally, I couldn't stand it. "Holly, when you were walking away from us last Sunday when we dropped you off, what were you thinking about?"

"Funny you should mention that," she said, "because I've been thinking about it all week. What went through my mind was, *Well, Mom and Dad really brought me up right, and now it's my turn to go do it.*"

Now it's my turn. I thought about her words then, and I still think about them now as I write this book. That's what being a good father is all about—training our daughters in the way in which they should go and then giving them their turn.

I got a note from Holly a few days later that included these words:

> Thanks for all your encouragement, Dad. Whenever I feel discouraged, I think of all the times you wanted to quit but didn't. Never forget how much you mean to me.
>
> I love you!
> Holly

When He Asks for Her Hand

There was a tone in his voice that tipped me off. It was the middle of October 1998. I was intently watching the University of Arizona football team battle the Washington Huskies. At half-time, Arizona was winning, and I was in a good mood.

Krissy's boyfriend, Dennis O'Reilly, noticed and decided it would be as good a time as any to let me know he was going to take my daughter away.

For life.

I walked into the kitchen and stopped short when Dennis asked, "Could I speak to you a second?"

Suddenly, the Leman females poured out of that kitchen as if someone had announced a plague. I might be dumb as mud some-times, but my radar isn't that dim. I knew something was going on.

Dennis got right to it. "I'd like to have Krissy's hand in marriage."

I grinned. I could make this easy . . . or hard. I knew all the girls were in the next room, listening through the door. All I'd have to do was yank the door open, and they'd fall into the kitchen. Talk about a public "private" conversation. I decided to make it easy and welcomed Dennis into the family. I knew he would be all right. He was a young man who, when his father died, quit school and worked for more than three years in a factory to support his family.

But inside, I was still swallowing hard. I remembered how much I didn't know when I married Sande, and that made me even more protective of Krissy, my first little bird to find a spouse.

Once again, my wife and I were on opposite sides of the spec-trum in our responses. I thought of my daughter getting married as a chapter that was closing. Sande insisted it was the reverse— an entirely new book opening for them, and for us.

What to Do and Not Do When Your Daughter Marries

- Don't ask what she's making for dinner (especially if she can't cook).
- Don't take sides in any disagreement. Memorize the words, "I'm sure you guys can handle it; I'm sure you'll work it out." That keeps you out of the line of fire and shows your positive expectation and confidence in them as a couple.
- Shut up until they ask.
- Don't give them money, unless they request help.
- Keep your nose in your own business.
- Ask about holiday visits. Don't tell.

When She Says, "I Do"

If any of you are dads who have married off daughters, you'll feel a shiver of fear when I say I have *four* daughters. As of the writing of this book, I've walked three of them down the aisle and still lived to tell about it. If you think it gets easier after number one, you're absolutely wrong. My family has developed a new word on my behalf: *setback.*

On March 27, 1999, Kleenex supplies dipped very low in Tucson, Arizona, as Krissy Leman changed her name to Kristin Leman O'Reilly. But the weeks before it were nearly as challenging.

"Let's talk about the wedding and make Daddy cry," became the new family sport.

Krissy showed me the wedding invitations. I cried.

She modeled her dress for me. I blubbered.

For weeks, she listened to various pieces of music to choose a wedding processional. Finally she chose a trumpet piece called "Trumpet Voluntary." I'd hear two bars of that composition and lose it. Hearing the piece brings mist to my eyes even today.

"Dad, are you going to be all right?" Krissy asked me. Understandably, she was concerned.

"Honey, I have one goal—to get down that aisle. After that, you're on your own. I'll be dead to the world," I managed.

So she made me start practicing with her at home. Suddenly, my knees would become like a bowl of oatmeal, and she had to hold me up.

"Have you considered a wheelchair?" I quipped. "Maybe you could push me down the aisle."

Concerned her old man would make a spectacle of himself on the most important day of her life, Krissy resorted to some psychological tactics of her own. She tried to "desensitize" me by making me watch *Father of the Bride*, a comedy starring Steve Martin, about a man surviving his daughter's wedding. The title and credits started rolling, and I lost it.

"Major setback," I choked out.

"I really thought we'd get past the words," Dr. Krissy Leman diagnosed. "You're worse off than I thought."

I know now that her two sisters who have since walked down the aisle—Hannah and Holly—completely agree with her. Big-time setback with both of their weddings too.

Sande was smart enough to insist I see Krissy's words to me on the program ahead of time:

> To my dad . . . From baby steps to walking me down the aisle, you have always held my hand, and you will always have my heart. I love you.

By the time Krissy's wedding weekend arrived, I was numb. I could identify very closely with Steve Martin in *Father of the Bride*. I had hand cramps from writing out checks, including one for a cake that cost $4.50 a slice, flowers, and even an ice sculpture that mysteriously showed up. But as I gathered in that church for the rehearsal, I saw everyone I treasure the most in one place:

> Krissy, the bride
> Lauren, our youngest, as the flower girl
> Hannah, our first "surprise" child, as a bridesmaid
> Kevin II, our son, as a groomsman
> Holly, as maid of honor
> Sande, my radiant bride of thirty-two years, beaming as
>   she watched our happy family interact

I couldn't help but think, *What more could a man want?*

At the Friday night rehearsal, knowing I was such a blubbering idiot, my family planned a surprise for me to lighten the moment. When Krissy and I started down the aisle on the practice run, everybody held up signs that said, *You're brave. You can do this.*

When I glanced up front, I couldn't help it. I started to laugh.

All my life, I've been the strength of our family. But that day, my kids and my wife held me up. Together, they were my strength. The mixture of feeling weak and strong at the same time was one of the most profound experiences I've ever known. I realized right then that there is nothing in life—absolutely nothing—that can mean more to a man than investing the time in family and having that investment returned.

During the wedding, something wonderful was born when

the pastor announced, "Mr. and Mrs. Dennis O'Reilly." I again felt the pangs of joy and sadness at life's transitions. During the father-bride dance, Krissy had picked out the song "My Father's Eyes," made popular back then by Amy Grant. It was a particularly meaningful song for us, as everyone has always said that Krissy got her long eyelashes and light brown eyes from me.

During the dance Krissy and I cried, laughed, and cried some more.

"Hey, Krissy," I said, "we've always had a special time together, haven't we? You've been such a wonderful daughter. I couldn't ask for a better daughter."

"And I'll always be your little girl," she answered back.

Holding her close, I whispered to her my hope that she would have the best marriage ever, and that she and Dennis would get to know each other well and share the ups and downs of life with grateful and faith-filled hearts.

Something happened in that moment. I had begun to let go ever since Krissy had announced her engagement, but this dance completed that task, as much as a father's heart is capable of letting go of his daughter. I remembered clearly the first time we left Krissy with a babysitter. A few years later, we let her spend an entire day at school. Next were the all-night stay-overs at Grandma's or a friend's house. Following that were the weeklong camps and then the more substantial partings of college. Every absence was a step to this road when Krissy would no longer be under my direct care.

I held Krissy tightly, but when the music stopped, I opened my arms and let her go. Krissy had found a new home with a man I was confident would love her and provide for her the rest of her life. The same young man

> Something happened in that moment.

who had quit school and worked for more than three years to provide for his mom and siblings when his father died.

Two nights after I took them to the airport, Sande and I tucked Hannah and Lauren in to bed. But this time, there was no Krissy to tuck in.

Yes, it was strange. Life had changed. It would never be the same again. But life was still good.

"Well," I told Sande, "I survived. I got through it."

Sande leaned over my shoulder. "And, to think, we only have to do this four more times," she whispered.

Making the Best of Your Time

I love how Stephen Covey said it: "Start with the end in mind." If you are rearing a daughter to someday be a wife, a mom, a professional, a good worker, or the best at whatever she decides to be, you need to start now by instilling qualities in her that will assist her in being successful in those roles. The best thing any man can do is be an actively, positively engaged daddy to his daughter. Men, we all have the same amount of hours in the day. Spending those hours wisely is what's most important.

So will you choose to knock out an extra project at work and earn a few more bucks? Or will you choose to say to your boss, "The extra money and hours sound great, but I promised my family I'd be home"? Dad, your daughter is waiting for you, even if it seems as if she doesn't pay much attention to you at times, especially when friends are around.

Leila, an active and confident fourteen-year-old, waits between six o'clock and six thirty every evening for the electronic sound of the garage door opening that alerts her that her dad is home. Then she races for the door to give him a hug and starts jabbering about her day. When she was younger, she used to crawl into a low kitchen cabinet to await his arrival, and he'd have to "find" her, which, of course, meant looking in a lot of other cabinets first while he hunted. "When my dad's home, I feel happy and safe," Leila says. "The couple times a year that he has to travel for his job I get antsy because home doesn't feel the same. Sometimes Mom lets me crawl under the covers and sleep with her."

See, Dad, how important you are? Isn't that worth sacrificing some golf outings while your daughter is growing up? Home is not the same without your presence. To your daughter, your presence means safety.

So, if you're a die-hard football fan, don't save that for the guys. Teach your daughter about football. Cuddle her right next to your side and explain the game to her; talk to her about her life during the commercials; plan special snacks. "One of my favorite memories is watching *Monday Night Football* with my dad," twenty-one-year-old Megan says. "I'd hurry to get my homework done, because it was our time. I'd hustle to get to the couch first, so I could sit right beside my dad, and almost always beat my brothers to the spot." Megan's first cooking experiment was baking a chocolate cake in the shape of a football to surprise her dad on his birthday.

> Home is not the same without your presence. To your daughter, your presence means safety.

If you like to play computer games, teach your daughter how to play. Then wait a year or less—she'll smoke you and your buddies. Mia's dad arranged computer-game weekends three times a year with his group of high school friends who were all still local. The guys came, slept over in sleeping bags, ate "guy food," and played games. At age four, Mia had her very own station and "played" right along with the guys in a special section of the game her daddy had blocked for her as safe. As an only child, Mia has learned how to relate to guys and watched how guys relate to each other (though she could do without the belching contests, she says) by growing up with this group of guys, who now feel like her uncles. At age thirteen, she's a game whiz, and the guys shake their heads at being bested by a girl. Next year she'll go into high school, able to confidently interact with boys and hold her own since she's used to being around males.

So take a look at your schedule, Dad. Are there things you regularly do that you think of as "guy only" where you could include your daughter? What activities could go, or lessen, that you do by yourself until she's grown up? Mark plays racquetball at a club with a coworker, but picks up his five-year-old daughter, Shelli, after work first. She watches his game, laughing when he misses a ball, and he reserves a few minutes at the end of his game to teach her how to play. On the way home they stop at Jamba Juice for smoothies. Shelli, a middle child, guards that Tuesday-night time with her dad jealously. A month ago, she chose it over an outing with a new kindergarten friend.

There's a lost art today called the "Dinner Table." It's a place where family members can come together to exchange information and feelings. It's designed to help the family become more cohesive. How often do you and your family make dinner together, with all members present, a priority? In the typical American family, individuals grab bits of food out of the refrigerator and pantry at different times, or go through a drive-through, eating on the run. They're like passing ships who give each other an occasional beep of the horn for communication. There's nothing like food to draw people into conversation. Everyone has to eat. Why not make it the happy event of the day that everyone wants to come to?

Plan special food. For you noncooks, it can be simple. The heart and intention behind it is what counts. Throw out fun discussion questions, talk about memories, and make memories. Most of all, laugh together. There's an old saying, "The family that plays together stays together." It's true. I'd add to it, "The family that plays together and laughs together stays together."

> There's a lost art today called the "Dinner Table."

Laughter truly is good medicine.

Our Dinner Date

I'm a single dad. I felt like I hadn't seen my two high school daughters in weeks because we all had different schedules. I heard you talk on the radio about the dinner table being an important way to draw families together. My first thought was, *But I can't cook.* Still, I told my girls I had a special dinner planned. They raised their eyebrows, but we set the dinner date for a night later that week. If you saw my girls' schedules, you'd know that was a major accomplishment. I picked up Chinese takeout, arranged it on our best plates, dug out their mother's linen napkins, and lit some candles. Emily and Faith were shocked, to say the least. That night we had one of the best conversations we've ever had. Three days later, I announced another family dinner. The girls walked into the kitchen and their jaws dropped. I was boiling spaghetti noodles, had made a salad (with more than one ingredient!), and had the kitchen bar set again with our best plates. Yeah, we had Ragu sauce on the spaghetti, but it didn't matter. My girls were hooked. Now we have our "Dinner Date" twice during the school week and once on the weekends. It's a big deal to us. Last week, the girls surprised me and they cooked. They did a much better job than I do! Most important, we're connecting again. I know their mother is looking down from heaven and smiling, watching us.

—Jerry, Ohio

If you want something to be different in your daddy-daughter connection, the time to start is now. Are too many activities in your life and her life keeping you apart? If so, it's time to get out the schedule trimmers and go to town.

Is your critical eye saying to your daughter, "You're not good enough. You'll never be good enough"? Then it's time for you to take a hard look at yourself and your expectations. For your relationship to change, you first have to change. Then you need to apologize to your daughter. Tell her you only now realized what you're doing—parenting like your critical-eyed father or mother did to you—and that you will work hard to change. Ask her to hold you accountable to do that, and her jaw will drop.

If you see areas in your daughter's life that you'd like to change, start by being a good role model yourself in those areas. Slip in those commercial announcements. For example, let's say you overhear your daughter making fun of other kids in school to her friends. If you confront her, you know she'll tell you, "Why do you care? That's my business."

Instead, you pull a smart-dad maneuver. Over dinner, you

casually say, "I learned something about myself today. At break time I caught myself talking bad about a coworker to another coworker . . . just when I'd vowed I'd never do that again. It's hard to change old habits, but I'm sure determined to work on them." Statements like that make your daughter think, because you, Dad, walk on water in her eyes. Right now she's processing. *Wait a minute. You mean my dad struggles with stuff like that too?* She's far more likely to admit her problems to you if you don't put yourself up on that "I'm perfect" pedestal.

Do you expect the best of your daughter? Do you trust her? Do you reveal that to her in your words and in your actions? One of the trickiest things about fathering is learning when to hold our daughters close and when to let them go. It's an ongoing process.

The greatest accomplishment you can ever undertake is preparing your daughter—the next generation—to take over her world. So give her a good start:

- Focus on the relationship that matters most to her: your daddy-daughter connection.
- Do what you can do, and don't bemoan what you can't.
- Get to know your daughter as an individual.
- Live a disciplined, balanced lifestyle yourself.
- Share with her your male perspective.
- Stay steady and calm in the heat of battle between those of the female gender.
- Keep an eye on your critical eye.
- Remember that your daughter doesn't need stuff. She needs you.
- Encourage and affirm her.
- Fine-tune your priorities to make the best of the time you have on this earth.

The simple facts are these:

You don't need a PhD to figure out your daughter, but you do need a listening ear.

You don't need to lie awake at night thinking about what you're not able to give your daughter. Instead, give her what you do have in abundance: the gift of yourself.

There's nothing your daughter wants more than a daddy-daughter connection.

A Good Dad's Quick Reference Guide

- Fine-tune your schedule.
- Create opportunities to interact with your daughter.

Conclusion

A Dad's Lasting Legacy

*You leave an indelible imprint on your
daughter's heart. What will yours be?*

There's no doubt that dads have a lifetime impact on their daughters. What do you want yours to be? You might be a young dad, or a planning-to-be-a-dad-soon guy, or one with a few gray hairs (or a lot) on your head. You might be one of those dads who has been able to hit on all eight cylinders with his daughter and only wants to tweak the carburetor a little. Or you might have realized, in the course of this book, that you are an MIA dad and want to change that. No matter where you are in your relationship, I guarantee that the daddy-daughter connection can grow stronger. You can make an indelible imprint on your daughter's heart. You can leave a lasting legacy for the next generation.

A Milestone Birthday Surprise

This week, as I worked to complete the manuscript for this book, I hit a milestone birthday. A big milestone. If you do the math of other references I've made to myself in this book, you'll be able to figure out which one it is. I say this because we men like to problem solve, so I'm helping you out by giving you a problem to solve.

As a baby of the family, I love surprises and celebrating events. My family knows that, so they go out of their way to surprise me. But I had no idea what they had up their sleeves this time, and my firstborn wife was keeping mum. I couldn't get a thing out of her. She even threw me a curveball. She scheduled a Mexican fiesta on Saturday night (let's say Mexican food isn't one of my favorites and leave it at that) and invited a few people over to fool me into thinking that was my birthday celebration. My editor even conspired with my wife to sidetrack me, arranging for the delivery of a huge rainbow of multicolored balloons to equal my birthday years during the fiesta. But the real deal was actually the next day.

More than fifty people—including my five kids and some close friends and colleagues—flew in from all over the nation to surprise me at a big hoopla at a local restaurant. I, Kevin Anderson Leman, was so surprised I was even tongue-tied for a minute. And that rarely happens. My son, Kevin II, masterfully played the role of emcee for his rendition of *Let's Make a Deal*, where he handed out prizes to our guests. The plan was to have Kevin start sharing about what I meant to him before his sisters got up and shared from their hearts. He tried on two occasions, and all he mustered up was a couple of sounds. He was so choked up, he couldn't say what was in his heart. But I did get the message: he loves his dad.

Part of the celebration was a DVD presentation that our daughter Hannah had pulled together. She'd asked people I knew from all walks of life to record a few words. Each of our kids also contributed. As I sat watching that DVD, I had another of those "setbacks," as my family calls it. I was overwhelmed, realizing the power that a single person can have over others' lives. And I was humbled to hear, from my kids' mouths, the indelible imprint I had made on their hearts.

Each of my daughters mentioned she was sure *she* was my favorite daughter and gave reasons. They all highlighted moments—both little and big—when I had made them feel unique and special. Here are a few of the things they mentioned:

HANNAH: Every Friday morning there was a pink box on the table with a chocolate éclair, and I knew that was from you, for me, because you knew that was my favorite. I treasure all my moments with my family, but the ones I remember most are those with just you and me, Dad. In a family so big those memories are so especially precious. My phone is programmed to say, "favorite daughter" when you call, and I think that says it all.

HOLLY: I'm your favorite, because you've known me the longest, so that gives me automatic points. Every Friday morning you'd always have a chocolate éclair waiting for me on the table, because you knew that's what I liked best. When I was very little, you'd wake me up and take me fishing with you. I hate fishing, but I loved being alone with you. You had an old rowboat with an outboard motor. I always hoped it started so we could go together. There was a peace, a calmness in those private moments with you. I never told you this before, but even now, on all the foggy, gray Tucson mornings, I think of those beautiful mornings on the lake with just you.

LAUREN: When I have any problems, you're the first person I call. I can always talk to you about anything. I appreciate that even more now, when a lot of my friends don't have that kind of a relationship with their fathers. I appreciate your generous and open heart and sense of humor. You always made me feel special. Every Friday you'd buy me doughnut with frosting and sprinkles. I'd know it was for me, because it was the only one like it, and you knew exactly what I liked. In fact, I made up a song for you based on all the little moments that have meant so much to me. . . .

KRISSY: When I heard it's a competition of who your favorite daughter is, I decided to go last, because it's in the bag. Holly is the brains; I could never compete with her report card. Lauren is extremely creative; she can make something out of nothing. Hannah has a compassionate heart for people who can't help themselves and travels to Africa; that's not me either. So what have I done that my other siblings haven't done? I've made you a grandpa. Watching you fall in love with my kids and watching my kids fall in love with you . . . wow, that's beyond describing. In regard to my own childhood, you and I are like two peas in a pod. I look just like you, and I get really feisty like you. One of the things I remember most is sitting in seventh grade toward the end of the day and hearing my name called over the loudspeaker. I had to go to the office. When I got there, you were there, and you said quietly to me, "Hey, we're outta here. Baseball. Me and you." We'd sit behind the dugout together. To this day, when I go there and see anyone sitting there, I think, *Hey, you're in my seat.* I grew up there, behind the dugout. On Friday, we all got our sweet treat from you. Mine was always a petit four. Dad, I love ya with all my heart. There's not a day that goes by when I don't thank God for a dad like you. That's how I know I'm your favorite.

Dad, I want you to imagine right now that your daughter is recording a DVD about you. What would you like to hear her say about your imprint on her heart and life? Why not tweak your relationship, starting today, with that end in mind?

Love That Man

I recently received one of the most touching e-mails I've ever received, and it was from my second cousin Carol—the youngest child of Carlton, my cousin twenty years my senior. She and her family grew up two streets from me, but she, her husband, Bob, and the kids now live in North Carolina. I have her permission to share the story below.

> Kevin, it was great to talk to you. It really warms my heart to hear all about your kids. It's so awesome that you are so close and loving. Makes me really miss those Andersons. [My mom was an Anderson, and they had nine kids in the family.] All the aunts and uncles were so cute. There were nine of them. I can't remember a family reunion where there weren't at least three of those cuties crying with happiness. Makes me really miss my dad too. Even though he could be a bit tough at times, he was such a great dad to me.
>
> Don't know if you know this, but my dad was in a home for the last few years. Bob, the boys, and I would go and visit him every week. His tiny room was filled with pictures the boys would draw for their "Papa." My dad had no idea who we were at that stage. Anyway, every time we would go to leave, he would cry and ask us to take him with us. He said even though he didn't know us, we seemed like real nice people. It would break my heart to leave him.
>
> The day after Easter I went to see him without Bob and the boys. I took him a really big chocolate bunny sucker and a chocolate shake—two of his favorites. As I walked into his room, there he sat, in some other person's clothing (this was typical), with his Velcro sneakers on the wrong feet.

I sat beside him and gave him his treats. He lit up like a four-year-old sitting on Santa's lap. I told him what the boys were up to, even though he had no clue who the boys were. When he finished the treats, there was chocolate all over his face. As I was cleaning his face, he looked at me.

All of a sudden he said, "You can go. I'm fine."

I laughed and said, "I'm not going anywhere."

He said it again, but this time almost like he knew what he was saying. This took me by surprise since he always cried when I left.

I told him, "Okay," gave him a hug and a kiss and told him I loved him. As I walked to the door to leave, my dad said to me, "Boy, I never thought I'd be treated this good today."

I smiled and told him I'd see him in a few days and left.

Ten minutes after I left, he died of a heart attack. I was the one they called. I'm positive he knew he was going to die and didn't want me to be there. My daddy even protected me to the end.

Love that man.

Now, do you think I could read that e-mail with dry eyes? Not on your life! I wept profusely, thinking about Carol and Carlton, her father—a man I also loved dearly and who was my favorite older cousin—and about my own relationships with each of my daughters. I want to protect them until the end too.

After all, that's what good dads do.

But note that I said "good dads," not "perfect dads." We all fail sometimes. I'm not a perfect dad, but I'm an involved, caring dad. I didn't always do the right things, but I have focused on building my relationship with my kids. And you know what? Being a good dad is enough. It has produced five amazing Leman kids. I'm so proud of each one of them.

Daughters who are secure in their daddy's love will be able to step confidently into life because they know Daddy is there for them, no matter what. Dads who love their daughters, affirm them, and encourage them produce daughters who do fine in school, who find careers that match their talents, and who make wise relational choices.

Those are only a few of the lasting legacies that you, and only you, can provide for your daughter.

What will your legacies be?

A Good Dad's Quick Reference Guide

- Engage in your daughter's life to stay in her heart.
- Be loving, steady, and balanced.
- Your girl isn't a boy.
- Your job: serve, protect, defend, take calculated risks, and problem-solve.
- Know and love your daughter as an individual.
- Make her feel special.
- Keep your cool.
- Balance always wins the game.
- Tell stories.
- Build your relationship.
- Stay calm.
- Side with Mama.
- Affirm instead of flaw-pick.
- Say "I love you" always and often.
- Say, "I'm sorry. Please forgive me."
- Make a plan for reconnecting.
- Walk your talk.
- Become the kind of man you'd want your daughter to marry.

- Affirm your daughter for who she is now.
- Give her freedom both to fail and to fly.
- Fine-tune your schedule.
- Create opportunities to interact with your daughter.

The ABCs of a Good Dad

Authentic, **A**vailable

Balanced

Caring, not **C**ritical

Disciplined in his own lifestyle

Encouraging, **E**xpects the best

Focuses on long-term goals

A **G**ood role model

Heart-connected to his daughter

Is always available

Never prioritizes **J**ob over family

Knows his duckling

An effective **L**istener

A **M**an, not a mouse

Never MIA

Open to suggestions about how to be a better father

A **P**rotector

Allows his **Q**ueen bee to do what she does best and acts as
   her helpmate and complement in doing what he does best

Focuses on **R**elationships over rules

Steady and calm in the heat of battle

Trustworthy

Unconditionally loving

Values his presence over presents

Walks his own talk

A permanent **X** marks the spot in his heart for his daughter

Says **Y**es whenever he can. Reserves no for the mountains of life.

Z _____ (You fill in the blank!)

Notes

Chapter 1: The Relationship That Matters Most

1. "Facts on Father Absence," National Fatherhood Initiative, accessed August 23, 2013, http://www.fatherhood.org/media /fatherhood-statistics.
2. If you want to know more of the effects—including child abuse, obesity, drug and alcohol abuse, and education—read more of this amazing study at "The Father Factor: Data on the Consequences of Father Absence and the Benefits of Father Involvement," National Fatherhood Initiative, accessed August 21, 2013, http://www.fatherhood.org/media/consequences -of-father-absence-statistics.
3. Nancy Fowler, "Joblessness, jail, death keep many black fathers out of the picture," The Art of Fatherhood, accessed August 23, 2013, https://www.stlbeacon.org/#!/content/26059/black _fatherhood_071612.

Chapter 2: Dads Do It ~~Better~~ Different

1. "O Be Careful Little Eyes," author unknown, http://childbiblesongs .com/song-12-be-careful-little-eyes.shtml, accessed August 15, 2013.

Chapter 3: Know Your Duckling

1. Eckhard H. Hess, "'Imprinting' in Animals," *Scientific American* 198:3 (March 1958): 81–90, accessed August 19, 2013, http://www.columbia.edu/cu/psychology/terrace/w1001 /readings/hess.pdf.

2. Ibid.

3. "Imprinting," AnimalBehaviour.net, http://animalbehaviour
   .net/Imprinting.htm, accessed August 21, 2013.

4. Ibid.

Chapter 4: Walking the Balance Beam

1. Lisa Belkin, "Your Lying, Cheating, Stealing Teens,"
   Motherlode (blog), *New York Times,* December 3, 2008, http://
   parenting.blogs.nytimes.com/2008/12/03/dirty-rotten
   -teenage-scoundrels.

2. Lisa Belkin, "Calling the Cops on Your Child," Motherlode
   (blog), *New York Times,* March 24, 2009, http://parenting.blogs
   .nytimes.com/2009/03/24/calling-the-cops-on-your-child/?_r=0.

3. Sir Walter Scott, "Marmion: A Tale of Flodden Field," *Canto
   Sixth: The Battle* (New York: Houghton Mifflin, 1884), 287.

Chapter 5: The Birds, the Bees, and "the Talk"

1. Genesis 2.

2. "Abduction Information," Heidi Search Center, accessed
   August 17, 2013, http://heidisearchcenter.com/abduction
   -information.

3. Adoree Durayappah, "5 Scientific Reasons Why Breakups Are
   Devastating," The Blog, *Huffpost Healthy,* August 18, 2013,
   http://www.huffingtonpost.com/adoree-durayappah-mapp
   -mba/breakups_b_825613.html.

Chapter 7: The Critical Eye

1. Robert Mark Kamen, Mark Miller, Harvey Weitzman, *A Walk
   in the Clouds,* directed by Alfonso Arau (Los Angeles: 20th
   Century Fox, 1995).

2. Felix Salten, Perce Pearce, and Larry Morey, *Bambi,* directed by
   David Hand (Hollywood, CA: Walt Disney Studios, 1942).

3. Gail Sheehy, *Hillary's Choice* (New York: Ballantine, 2000), 22.

4. Ibid., 28, 22.

5. Hillary Rodham Clinton, *It Takes A Village,* 10th anniversary
   ed. (New York: Simon & Schuster, 2006), 32.

6. Sheehy, *Hillary's Choice,* 23.

Chapter 8: A Cake Without Sugar

1. Sue Kidd, "Don't Let It End This Way," reprinted in *Focus on the Family*, January 1985.

Chapter 9: Are You a Man or a Mouse? Squeak Up!

1. Alan Ebert, "Fathers and Daughters," *Good Housekeeping*, June 1992.
2. Ibid.
3. Ibid.

Chapter 10: If You See a Turtle on a Fencepost . . .

1. Taylor Swift, vocal performance of "You Belong with Me," by Taylor Swift and Liz Rose, http://www.youtube.com/watch?v =VuNIsY6JdUw, accessed September 6, 2013.
2. Taylor Swift, "I Knew You Were Trouble," by Taylor Swift, Max Martin, and Shellback, http://www.youtube.com/watch?v =vNoKguSdy4Y, accessed September 6, 2013.
3. Robert Goldman and Stephen Papson, *Nike Culture: The Sign of the Swoosh* (Thousand Oaks, CA: Sage Publications, 1998), 49.

Chapter 11: Time Is Tickin'

1. DC Talk, "Time Is . . . ," http://www.lyricstime.com/dc-talk -time-is-lyrics.html, accessed August 16, 2013.

About Dr. Kevin Leman

An internationally known psychologist, radio and television personality, speaker, educator, and humorist, Dr. Kevin Leman has taught and entertained audiences worldwide with his wit and commonsense psychology.

The *New York Times* bestselling and award-winning author of more than fifty titles, including *The Birth Order Book, Have a New Kid by Friday,* and *Sheet Music,* has made thousands of house calls through radio and television programs, including *Fox & Friends, The Real Story, The View,* Fox's *The Morning Show, Today, Morning in America, 700 Club,* CBS's *The Early Show, Janet Parshall,* CNN, and *Focus on the Family.* Dr. Leman has also served as a contributing family psychologist to *Good Morning America* and frequently speaks to schools and businesses, including Fortune 500 companies such as YPO, Million Dollar Round Table, Top of the Table, and other CEO groups.

Dr. Leman's professional affiliations include the American Psychological Association, SAG-AFTRA, and the North American Society of Adlerian Psychology.

He received the Distinguished Alumnus Award (1993) and an honorary doctor of humane letters degree (2010) from North Park University.

Dr. Leman earned his bachelor's, master's, and doctorate

degrees in psychology from the University of Arizona, where he was also given the Alumni Achievement Award in 2003. Dr. Leman is the founder and chairman of the board of the Leman Academy of Excellence (www.lemanacademy.com). Originally from Williamsville, New York, Dr. Leman and his wife, Sande, live in Tucson, Arizona. They have five children and four grandchildren.

For information regarding speaking availability, business consultations, and seminars, please contact:

Dr. Kevin Leman

P.O. Box 35370

Tucson, Arizona 85740

Phone: (520) 797-3830

www.birthorderguy.com

www.drleman.com

Follow Dr. Kevin Leman on Facebook (Facebook.com /DrKevinLeman) and Twitter (@DrKevinLeman). Check out the free podcasts at birthorderguy.com/podcast.

Resources by Dr. Kevin Leman

Nonfiction Books for Adults

Have a New Kid by Friday
The Birth Order Book
Have a Happy Family by Friday
Have a New Sex Life by Friday
Planet Middle School
Have a New Husband by Friday
Have a New Teenager by Friday
Have a New You by Friday
The Way of the Wise
Be the Dad She Needs You to Be
What a Difference a Mom Makes
Parenting Your Powerful Child
Under the Sheets
Sheet Music
Making Children Mind without Losing Yours
It's Your Kid, Not a Gerbil!
Born to Win
Sex Begins in the Kitchen
7 Things He'll Never Tell You . . . But You Need to Know

What Your Childhood Memories Say about You
Running the Rapids
The Way of the Shepherd (written with William Pentak)
Becoming the Parent God Wants You to Be
Becoming a Couple of Promise
A Chicken's Guide to Talking Turkey with Your Kids
about Sex (written with Kathy Flores Bell)
First-Time Mom
Step-Parenting 101
Living in a Stepfamily without Getting Stepped On
The Perfect Match
Stopping Stress before It Stops You
Single Parenting That Works
Why Your Best Is Good Enough
Smart Women Know When to Say No

Fiction Books for Adults, with Jeff Nesbit

The Worthington Destiny
A Perfect Ambition
A Powerful Secret
A Primary Decision

DVD Series for Group Use

Have a New Kid by Friday
Making Children Mind without Losing
Yours (parenting edition)
Making Children Mind without Losing
Yours (public school teacher edition)

Value-Packed Parenting
Making the Most of Marriage
Running the Rapids—Helping Your Teen
Survive the Turbulent Waters of Adolescence
Single Parenting That Works
Bringing Peace and Harmony to the Blended Family

DVDs for Home Use

Straight Talk on Parenting
Have a New Kid by Friday
Designer Sex

Available at www.drleman.com or by
calling (800) 770-3830 or (520) 797-3830.